# We Grow Kids Here

Essays on Life and Love in a Small Town

## STACEY MARTIN

# DEDICATION

For Mom and Dad.
Thanks for raising us in the best small town in America
and teaching us that we can always come back home.
Buchanan Forever!

# CONTENTS

# THE FOLKS BACK HOME

# Forward

This book is a collection of essays written mostly during the years of 2015-16 to capture the essence of growing up in a small-town and returning home to raise my own children. What originally started as a few long posts on social media chronicling daily life soon morphed into a blog with a substantial following and additional writing opportunities with local and national publications.

My stories focus on common themes of life, love, family, and small-town pride. You don't have to grow up here to appreciate the commonalities we all share and connect with the universal truths in parenting, relationships, and everyday life.

Thank you for picking up a copy of my book. I hope you'll enjoy reading my stories as much as I enjoyed living them.

And if you picked up a copy because of the beautiful cover, that's all thanks to my talented little sister, Bear. Follow Caryn DeFreez on Instagram to enjoy her documentary style photography.

# BIG LIFE IN A SMALL TOWN

It was nearly impossible to go for a walk as a kid in my hometown. It wasn't because I was worried about traversing through dangerous neighborhoods or being picked up by kidnappers in creepy vans with tinted windows. It wasn't due to heavy traffic caused by busy roads. My town has a total of four stoplights and one of those just graduated from blinking a few years ago. And it certainly wasn't because I didn't have any place to go—that is, if you count an empty parking lot behind a gas station as a destination worthy of gathering with friends.

What made this pursuit impossible was the sheer number of times my walk would be interrupted by a well-meaning driver who'd pulled over to ask if I needed a ride home. After reassuring them that I was simply getting a little exercise (and promising that I'd tell my Mom they'd said hi), I would carry on again only to be stopped 50 paces later by my great-aunt or my best friend's dad or my 6th grade teacher and be forced to repeat it all over again. After the fourth or fifth Good Samaritan stopped to offer a ride, I would finally give up, hop in the car, and catch a lift back home…usually just 15 minutes after I'd left.

That's the thing about small towns. Everybody knows everybody, and they all make a habit of looking out for one another. As teenagers from small towns across America know, this can be both a blessing and a curse. Lock your keys in your car at the grocery store? No worries, the town's locksmith will be up in a jiffy to help you out (for the second time this month) before your dad can even find your spare at home. Hit a homerun in the season opener? Prepare to be congratulated by every other person you see at the farmer's market the following weekend. Planning on throwing a party for forty of your closest friends while your parents are out of town? Kind of hard to do when they find out about it before they even leave the driveway. I'm sure you get the message: secrets are merely suggestions in a small town.

It's a bit ironic that what bugged me back then is one of many things that compelled me to return and raise my own kids here. I appreciate the comfort that comes with knowing the families of my kids' friends, having grown up with most of them myself. The first friend I ever met in elementary school was a cute little girl with short blonde hair and emerald green earrings. We sat next to each other on the first day of school and were inseparable from that moment on. We had sleepovers and play dates (before they were called that) and skipped down the soccer field, hand-in-hand, instead of worrying about silly things like kicking the ball or scoring goals. We remained friends even after our paths led us to different colleges and different stages in life. Fast forward more than a few years later to the day my son returned home from his first day of pre-school to tell me all about his very first friend. He was a cute little boy with a head full of blonde curls who sat in the desk right next to his and had a name that sounded very familiar. These two have been buddies ever since and it sure is fun to have an excuse to hang out with my first friend again while our sons are shooting hoops out in the driveway. You just can't get that kind of continuity in a big city.

I think it's the slower pace of life in a small town that draws many of us back as well. I'll never forget the time I brought a few of my big city college friends back home with me during one of our breaks. We were driving down the main street in town, and as we pulled up to one of the four stoplights, my friend noticed the vehicle ahead of us and shockingly asked, "Is that someone driving a tractor…like on the road…in town?" Not an unlikely occurrence in these parts, I looked over to confirm and, in doing so, noticed that not only was there a tractor stopped at the red light, but my cousin Perry was the one driving it. He waved, I waved back, and my friends erupted in laughter at what must've seemed to them like a scene right out of Mayberry. I didn't know what was so funny-- seemed like a pretty normal day to me.

I thought about the many aspects of my future life and the type of parent I'd want to be in the years before I had my children. I knew I wanted to expose them to great literature and encourage them to explore whatever talents and interests they possessed. I was determined to take them to see the country and wanted them to be open to new adventures. After all, I'd traveled and lived in numerous places after leaving the nest and I was sure my children would be just fine wherever they were planted.

And then I got pregnant.

During those nine months it seemed like the more I thought about my baby the more I wanted to just go home. I landed a job teaching at my old high school and moved back just a few months before my son was born.

In doing so, I made a conscious choice to replace "cutting-edge" with community. My kids will wear maroon and white and cheer for the Bucks just like I did, and just like my parents did. They will run around with friends who are also cousins and play on soccer teams coached by our former teammates. They will get the same purple personalized notes sent home from their elementary principal that I still have tucked away in my own dusty scrapbooks, the ones with a special note of recognition for all A's on a report card or a tremendous talent show performance and punctuated with a hand-drawn pig with a curly tail. They will probably spend their summers at the little league field down by the railroad tracks, where we spent much of our youth, and return foul balls to the concession stand for a piece of gum. They will sled down the same hill, splash through the same creek, hike through the same woods, and fall in love with the same town that I did. They will be big fish in a small pond, and that kind of confidence will serve them well whenever they decide to venture out into the big ocean.

It's true that we don't have the most "cultured" environment or the most exciting nightlife to offer here in our little corner of the world. We don't have a cinema or a shopping mall, and we aren't a stop on any metro-line. We don't even have a bowling alley or a place to get Thai food. You won't find a parking meter downtown or much rush-hour traffic either. Instead of riding the subway to a rock concert, our kids ride in pickup trucks to the county fair. We might not catch the latest fashion trends, but we sure catch a lot of bluegills. And forget weekends spent at sushi bars and art museums— Friday nights are for bonfires, Saturday afternoons are for ball games, and Sunday evenings are for family dinner at Grandma's house. We might not draw crowds of thousands to music festivals or city celebrations, but we can pack the downtown for our Spring Chili-Walk, and you should see all the folks who come back to town for the Homecoming game.

No, you won't find any gourmet food trucks on our tree lined streets, but you can get a dang good burger from the B&W, a killer omelet from Hilltop Cafe, a heartburn special from Milano's Pizza, and a bag of free popcorn from the Redbud Hardware. And, while I'm at it, you can keep your Starbucks;

we prefer our steamy beverages from Union Coffee House.

But what we lack in worldliness, we make up for in kindness. While we will never be described as cosmopolitan, you can't mistake our strong sense of community. I'm sure glad I decided to come back home. Dorothy was right: there really is no place like it.

# WE GROW KIDS HERE

The four ingredients necessary for an amazing summer are the exact same four ingredients required to sustain plant life: water, sun, air, and soil. Children and plants, if given those four things, will thrive during the hottest months of the year. We adults tend to require a few more ingredients to get by. We like to add fancy art projects and expensive sports camps, required reading time, and structured play dates. We like to complicate things that don't always need to be complicated. We overschedule, overcommit, and overdo. We could learn a thing or two from dandelions and our little ones.

Today I watched as 100 kids splashed through a field that was turned into a giant puddle by a fire truck spraying a constant stream of water overhead. A hillbilly splash pad, if you will. Our local library and our city fire department sponsor the annual 'Splash Day,' and it is always a big hit. The truck's water made a giant cascading arch under which the children ran, slid, jumped, splashed, chased, and laughed for a full hour. It was one heck of a sprinkler. Everywhere I looked, there were barefooted children covered in grass, soaked from head to toe, and grinning from ear to ear. Groups of friends who hadn't seen each other since school let out in early June were reunited for an afternoon. Younger brothers and sisters who tentatively followed their older siblings around at the beginning of the hour soon grew brave and ventured out to jump in their own puddles. Little girls held hands and screamed as they ran to the middle. Little boys competed to see who could slide the farthest on their bellies in the mud.

The closest thing to a planned activity or a structured event occurred when the guys who work for the city (dads and uncles themselves) pulled up to the field in an ATV loaded down with water balloons to pass out to the kids. There weren't any instructions to go along with the handout. The kids weren't required to line up and play catch with them or even wait in line to get their balloon. It was a free-for-all both during and after the handout--and it was awesome. Five minutes of an all-out, take-no-prisoners water balloon war, reminiscent of the epic dodgeball games played in gym class back in the good old days—before safety concerns and overbearing adults got in the way of all the fun.

My greatest summer memories growing up contain those same ingredients. Many hot days were spent at the beach with my mom and dad, uncles and aunts, siblings and cousins. We would pack a cooler and stay for hours, digging moats and swimming to the sandbar. I remember building giant sandcastles and adding embellishments with items we found on the beach: driftwood for drawbridges, rocks for walkways, and old cigarette butts for staircases. There was no structure to the day besides the obligatory hike up the sand dune. And we only brought one toy--a football to play catch in the lake.

As we got older, we rolled out our towels farther down the beach from our parents, basking in the sun and a tiny bit of freedom. One particular memory involves my best friend and I when we were 13 years old, sitting on our towels about 20 yards away from my dad who had volunteered to be our chauffeur and chaperone for the day (a thankless job when you are dealing with teenage girls). My little sister soon joined us and was receiving a first-hand lesson in gossip when we saw two cute boys headed in our direction. My friend leaned over and whispered, "*Let's tell them we're 16.*" And in the same low voice and with all sincerity, my nine-year-old sister added, "*Tell 'em I'm 10.*"

That's what you do when you have all the right ingredients—you grow. You dig your toes into the earth, and you plant your feet on solid ground. You gain strength and energy from the rays of the sun, and you lift your face toward its warmth. You find renewal in the cleansing power of the rain and learn to dance in it too. The warm breeze that carries the smell of lilacs and lavender can chase away even the biggest worries. Ah, to have many summers is a privilege denied to many, and its simple pleasures are enjoyed by too few.

There is an organic beauty in a minimalistic summer composed of those four life-sustaining ingredients. God knew what He was doing when He sent the soft summer rain to cool off the dog days of July and the sun's afternoon encore to dry the blades of grass for the evening picnic. Should you doubt the power of those four simple elements on the demeanor of your children, simply hook a cheap sprinkler up to an old garden hose and place it out in your yard. Then sit back in your lawn chair and watch the magic happen. No need to coordinate or orchestrate. They will leap and race and slide and giggle all on their own. The less intervention the better. Kids and trees grow best when they have the space to stretch out their branches.

A few years back, we were spending a late summer evening with family at a relative's house while my grandfather was spending his last days surrounded by those who loved him the most. My grandpa was a man who lived his life outdoors and instilled a love of nature in many of his descendants. From him I learned how to make maple syrup, boil sassafras tea, identify a Dogwood tree (by its bark), and call back to a katydid. We spent thousands of hours walking through trails in the woods or fishing in a canoe or just sitting on the grass talking. He didn't need much more than water, soil, air, and sun to make life worth living and to make memories with his grandkids.

While we kept a round-the-clock watch by his bedside, a few of the adults ventured outside in the cool air to watch the kids stretch their legs in a fierce game of freeze tag. In the midst of the match, some of the kids trampled right through my Aunt Marcia's beautiful flower bed. The parents quickly made a move to reprimand their children, but before they could get out a full sentence, my Aunt (and my grandpa's sister) turned to the parents and said, "*Let those babies be, they aren't hurting anything. We grow kids here, not flowers.*"

You bet we do.

We grow kids here.

We grow right along with them too. And, if we're lucky, we will get to enjoy many summers growing together. We don't need all the trappings of the modern world to enjoy it either. All we need is already outside our front door. A sunburned nose

and dirty toes, windblown hair and water
everywhere, proof of a life well lived.

# PINK CARNATIONS AND PICKUP TRUCKS

You couldn't have picked a better backdrop for the start of a love story. Surrounded by corn stalks and fertilizer, young love took root and grew into a field of dreams. My parents met in FFA class in high school. For those of you not from the Midwest area of the country, FFA stands for Future Farmers of America. This was (and in some places still is) an actual class held on the School's Farm that taught kids how to plant and harvest crops and take care of animals. My Dad tells a story of how they first met by recounting lifting my Mom up and placing her on top of a tractor.

Right then and there, the country boy fell hard for a small-town girl. When they talk about their high school romance, the story plays out in my head like a scene out of Footloose--all pink carnations and pick-up trucks. My mom, a woman who has never had a speeding ticket in her life, would spend every morning keeping my dad company as he sat in the hallway outside of the principal's office, serving a perpetually renewing detention. And my dad, a rebel in red flannel, would spend all of his graduation money on a little diamond ring that still graces my mother's left hand.

A year after they graduated, they got married. The pictures of that sweltering June day show two young kids, one in a long-sleeved lace wedding dress, the other in a brown tux, madly in love and ready to take on the world. It was 1980, and long, feathered back hair was in style for both men and women. What I'm trying to say is that my Mom and Dad had matching haircuts on their wedding day. That's either real love, real funny, or both.

Six days before their one-year anniversary, they had me. We spent the early years in a tiny apartment, devoid of many creature comforts but overflowing with love and warmth. My Dad drove truck and my mom worked as a secretary, so there wasn't a lot of expendable income. One year, we couldn't afford to buy a big Christmas Tree, so we found a two-foot-tall Charlie Brown Christmas Tree look-a-like. My mom and I made paper decorations at the kitchen table and proudly displayed our homemade creations on its branches. A few hours later, we heard a knock at the door, and my parents' best friends were standing in the doorway with a beautiful six-foot blue spruce in hand. I can neither confirm nor deny if said tree was cut down from an out-of-towner's beautifully landscaped yard. Either way, the statute of limitations has surely run out by now, so ignore the misdemeanor and enjoy the heartfelt sentiment behind the gift. This was my life growing up. Limited means but unlimited love.

When my sister was born a few years later, the family moved into a trailer placed on a cement slab on my grandparents' wooded property out in the country. To the untrained eye, it probably looked like a hardscrabble existence. But, to my sister and me, it was paradise. Sure, the deck that my Dad built was crooked and, yes, farm cats would randomly pop their heads up through the vents in the floors looking for food. But the epic wiffleball games in our front yard would bring country kids from miles around and, in the winter, all of the uncles and cousins would spend Saturday mornings shoveling off the pond below the hill to play a helmetless game of ice hockey. I'm not sure how many broken bones and broken noses came off that ice, but I do know that the frozen playground produced a lifetime of campfire worthy stories. In the days before helicopter-parenting and sunscreen, we roamed the woods with our gangs of friends. We climbed trees, played kick-the-can, made homemade weapons from branches, and stayed out after dark. And in the evening, we would sit around the fire and listen to my dad and his buddies tell stories about the good ole days while my mom made sure we had warm food in our bellies and soft pillows to sleep on. It was a simple life, but a charmed one.

Before my fifth-grade year, my parents loaded my sister and me into our old station wagon and drove us into town. They stopped at a small little green house, parked the car in the driveway, and told us to go inside for a look at our new house. When I think about the pride that my mom and dad must have felt in purchasing their first home, after years of saving and planning, my heart almost bursts. And so, the country mice moved to the suburbs. We became part of a neighborhood and created friendships that last until this day. We had lemonade stands and sleepovers and even bigger wiffleball games in the side yard. My best friend and I drove the riding lawnmower between our houses before we were old enough to drive our own cars. Our home was, once again, the gathering place. My Mom and Dad spent their hard-earned money paying electricity bills and feeding the hungry teenagers who managed to take over their couches every weekend.

The tradition continued years later as I left for college and my parents moved back to the country, surrounded by woods to hunt and a river to fish. They welcomed an ever-growing family to their old farmhouse and hosted Fourth-of-July parties and

Halloween trail walks. They also welcomed my little brother, nineteen years after they first became parents. When I think back to those days, my mind always pictures a three-year-old boy hiding behind a tree in the backyard, wearing nothing but his underwear and yellow rain boots, surveying the land with his BB gun, hoping for an unsuspecting turkey or buck to cross his path. And I can still see our dad, sitting in a lawn chair, softly chuckling at this sight of his mighty hunter with our Mom sitting next to him, eyes sparkling with love for her last-born baby. If you ever get a chance to meet this little boy, now a fourteen-year-old freshman in the same high school where his parents first met, it won't take long to see that he has his mother's kind heart and his father's love of the great outdoors.

It's been 35 years since those two crazy kids exchanged their vows and drove off in a red Trans Am with tin cans hanging off of the back bumper and "Just Married" written with white paint on the window. They defied the odds and quieted the doubters. They created a safe haven and a foundation for countless members of their tribe. They raised three children and spoiled six grandchildren. They proved that you can build a life on a little bit of money and a whole lot of love.

So, here's to young love everywhere. To the high school sweethearts and the hometown honeys.

To letterman jackets and brown tuxedos. To the girls-next-door and pink carnations. To sharing a slow dance at the senior prom that turns into a waltz down the aisle. To rocking by each other on the front porch fifty years after sitting by each other in math class.

Here's a little ditty 'bout Jack and Diane…or Paul and Joann. Theirs is the kind of love that people write stories about.

# TELL ME A STORY

I've always been a sucker for a good story. I blame this weakness of mine on a childhood filled with expertly spun tales. As a little girl, I would ride along in the cab of my dad's semi-truck and listen as he tuned in to *Gunsmoke* and *The Shadow* on crackly AM radio stations. During sleepovers at my grandma's house, she would pop in a worn-out cassette tape, and we would snuggle up in fuzzy blankets on the couch and listen as Garrison Keillor transported us to *Lake Wobegon*. Countless summer nights of my youth were spent gathered around a campfire, soaking up the stories of my elders and trying out a few of my own. I loved hearing about my grandpa's days as a lifeguard on Silver Beach, my dad's adventures on a fishing boat in Alaska, and my uncles' accounts of life aboard a naval ship, complete with colorful characters and more than a little rabble rousing. It's safe to say I'm smitten with the spoken word. If you have a story to tell, I'll plunk right down crisscross applesauce and follow along as you set the scene.

But if I had to nail down the origin of my obsession, I would choose the time my high school history teacher, Mrs. Ruth Writer, assigned me to interview the older members of my family. The purpose of the assignment was to record first-hand accounts of American history through the eyes of the Greatest Generation, but the discussion morphed into something much bigger than an A in the grade-book. A project that was intended to take thirty minutes of my time turned into a three-hour conversation around the dining room table with my great grandmother, four grandparents, multiple uncles and aunts, and a video recorder. What unfolded was an oral history of my family tree, a priceless collection of memories and moments all caught on tape and forever saved for posterity.

It was during this interview that I discovered that my sassy old grandma used to sell moonshine to the sheriff during Prohibition. I learned that my great-great-grandfather escaped from Sweden at 13 years old and stowed away on a ship bound for America. I found out that my grandma took care of her baby brother while the rest of her family picked cotton in an Arkansas field and that their sharecropping days ended when they received news of available factory jobs in the north. The most ordinary people have the most extraordinary stories to tell, if we'd only just ask them.

I witnessed this basic human instinct to share a connection play out in my classroom. My communications class had been working on a storytelling unit, and I'd called in a local expert to spin them a tale. To be honest, I didn't know what to expect. My students are teenagers who've grown up on electronics and instant gratification; they are a part of the YouTube generation, and they'd much rather text than talk. My speaker was Mrs. Canfield, a grandmother who specializes in Native American folktales and old-world charm. Would she be able to tell a story that would reach them? Would they lose interest or tune out? I watched with bated breath as she started in on a legend about a turtle, and within moments of uttering her first word, she had them. I knew it, and she knew it. For the next ten minutes, she transported them to a fabled land filled with changing voices and compelling characters. I sat back and marveled at their transfixed faces and delighted in their emotional reactions to every curve and twist of the narrative. And when the story was over, they wanted to know more. In their remaining time together, they asked for her advice: how could they become storytellers like her? Imagine that—a class full of millennials in love with an art form older than the first Nintendo. They might be onto something.

So is it the storyteller or the story itself that draws us in and holds us hostage to the rise and fall of the plotline? Based on my non-scientific data collection and far-from-expert opinion, I think the answer is both. But in all my research there seems to be one common denominator—an undeniable connection that is formed between young and old through a shared story that includes relevant themes for all generations. The reason I loved listening to the adventures of my elders is because it left me wishing for adventures of my own someday. Their experiences only served to heighten their status around the campfire. Granny suddenly earns a lot of street cred when the grandkids find out she was at Woodstock.

Now I usually don't give homework, but this time I'm making an exception. I'm encouraging you to learn a little more about those you love the most. Be thankful that you have grandparents sitting around the dining room table at the next family dinner and ask them a question or two about their lives before you arrived on the scene. Chances are you'll still be laughing by the time the chocolate cream pies are passed around. If you are a grandparent, give thanks for the beautiful children running around the house and gather them all in front of your rocking chair for a tale from your younger years. At some point, and before it's too late, take the often-missed opportunity to connect through conversation. Replace the ubiquitous HD screens with actual faces and *real* definition. Tell a story. Listen to a story. And record it; you'll thank me later.

# THE BEAUTY OF BOREDOM

"*Mom, what else are we doing today besides going to the movies, going swimming, and going to see fireworks?*" I almost spit out my coffee. What else? What else besides dropping $40 on the latest Pixar flick, serving lifeguard duty for 3 hours, and then packing up a cooler of snacks and a tote of playground equipment and heading out to a field with 30 of our closest relatives to watch the night sky fill with colorful explosions? It was right then and there that I realized that my kids have a problem. They are having too much fun. And it is (mostly) my fault.

Now don't get me wrong, I am not anti-fun. It's just the "too much" fun that I am starting to think is a problem. Perhaps I should provide some context. Within the past week, my kids have enjoyed the following activities: a trip to the zoo with 14 of their cousins, a swimming party at their Nana and Papa's, a ride in a parade, a day at a kids museum followed by fun at a splash pad, a movie with their dad, fireworks, gymnastics, hockey camp, countless games of wiffle ball, a run through the sprinklers with more cousins, two community events sponsored by our local library, and a sleepover with (you guessed it) even more cousins. This schedule is not atypical. In fact, it's pretty standard for our family this summer.

Many of you are probably wondering, "Why is this a problem? This seems like the makings of a wonderful childhood!" And you are correct. Mostly. It's just that, with all of this fun (scheduled and spontaneous), I'm worried that my children aren't learning how to enjoy a 'normal' day. On days when there isn't a carnival going on in their world, will they know how to occupy their time? Are they capable of curing their own boredom? I'm running a household, not a cruise ship. And I need them to know the difference.

I remember having a lot of fun as a kid during the summer. I recall long days spent playing in the woods or rounding up the neighborhood for 15 innings of kickball. I recollect the slumber parties and the water parks. If I think hard enough, I can still smell the campfires and picture the fireflies from those hot July nights. But I also remember long days of doing nothing. Of spending sun up to sundown with only the characters of the Babysitter Club to keep me company.

Boredom, like youth, is wasted on the young. What I wouldn't give for a boring day! Can you imagine the luxury of not having to do anything for 24 whole hours? No making breakfast for picky children, no folding laundry or running errands, no appointments, no bath time shenanigans or bedtime routines? An entire day of staying in your pajamas (and in bed), reading, watching TV, or just (dare I say it) sleeping! It sounds amazing...and when that day comes, ten years from now, I will be ready to do nothing.

Growing up, whenever my sister or I would lodge that age-old complaint of boredom to our parents, my dad would always respond with, "*Only boring people get bored.*" The sheer brilliance of that response still amazes me to this day, and I'd be lying if I said that I haven't already used it a time or two on my own children. Think about the complexity of that statement. Not only was my dad trivializing our boredom (which, put into a worldly context, the boredom of first-world children is trivial), but he was also placing it squarely on us. It wasn't his responsibility to entertain us. If we were bored, that was our problem. And by us owning the problem, we also had to learn how to come up with a solution. Not to mention the fact that our character was called into question. I would always come away from that response with the thought, *"Am I a boring person? I don't want to be a boring person. I better find something to do so that I'm not bored and, by extension and even worse, boring."* Brilliant.

So, we read books and wrote stories, rearranged our rooms and made up games, learned how to enjoy the silence and appreciated the stillness. The outside world was ours to explore, and we only needed to bring our imagination. On these "boring" days, our favorite game to play was space pig. We would sit on top of the white propane tank in the yard with the cap on the end that looked like a pig snout and pretend that we were blasting into outer space and exploring the galaxy. Another favorite activity was "Leader of the Pack" – a game that involved getting on our motorcycles (bikes), revving our engines (handlebars), and riding in circles on our old country road with our gang (cousins).

I want my kids to be able to do this. I want them to have fun-filled days spent at locations that require an admission ticket, but I want those days to be interspersed among days where they don't leave the house. Days at the museum or the theme park should feel special. Sleepovers with a floor full of cousins and friends should be something to look forward to. Real life mixes the mundane with the magnificent. Besides, without Mondays, we wouldn't enjoy the weekends nearly as much.

So when my kids wake up tomorrow morning and ask, *"What are we going to do today Mom?"*, I am going to respond with one word--*"Nothing."* Their faces will probably break into expressions of disappointment and sadness. They will probably comment on how boring a day of nothingness sounds. For added enjoyment, they might even stomp around in a true display of spoiled kid syndrome. But then, with a little luck, they might venture upstairs to check out a long forgotten toy. It's possible they will dig Twister or Connect 4 out of the game chest and challenge each other to a round or two. Perhaps the cushions on the couch will become the four walls of a newly constructed fort. Maybe, just maybe, they will invent a new game involving hot lava, stuffed animal bombs, and pirate costumes. Pretend might replace planned today--and I might be able to get some laundry done.

# SEARCHING FOR GREENER PASTURES

The two boys appeared in my peripheral vision as I sat at the family's dining room table, suddenly visible through the sliding glass door leading out onto the back deck. I watched as the older brother carried the younger one up the hill, slung over his shoulder like a sack of potatoes with his backpack hanging down to the side. It was so unexpectedly comical that I laughed out loud. Their mother, sitting next to me at the table, smiled proudly and chuckled as well. These farm boys, muscles strong from daily chores, walked through the maze of chickens greeting them in the yard, up the deck stairs, and through the sliding door to address me with manners that you don't often see these days. As I got a hug from the youngest and a handshake from the oldest, one thing was abundantly clear:

their parents were doing a great job raising these two young men.

These days, however, Sean and Alejandra Finn are doing much more than raising their two sons: Nicholas (10) and Matthew (8). Three years ago, the Finn family packed up their belongings and moved from the South side of Chicago to a farmhouse in Buchanan. They traded a suburban neighborhood for 14 acres of land and replaced the convenience of city life with a dirt road and a pasture full of cows. They took a chance on a new way of life, and, by all accounts, it was a pretty good bet. During my recent visit to Finn's Steak and Eggs Ranch, I learned that sometimes the best things in life aren't exactly planned.

As Sean gave me a walking tour of the grounds, he explained the origin of the newly formed ranch. In 2012, Sean was relocated by his employer of 22 years, Kennicott Brothers (a floral distribution company) from the Chicago area to an office in South Bend. In planning for the big move, the couple looked at homes in the Granger area but couldn't find anything that seemed like a good fit. One Sunday afternoon they took a drive around southwestern Michigan to get a feel for the area and turned down a little dirt road on the West side of Buchanan. They noticed a charming farmhouse on a hill with a sale sign in the yard. On a whim, they called the agent listed on the sign for more information, and she arrived within minutes to let them inside. According to Alejandra, they fell in love with the home and the surrounding land instantly. And so it began--their transition from the city to the country. Little did they know, however, that the decision to turn down that dirt road would change more than just their mailing address.

As Sean tells it, the big move started out innocently enough. He continued to work in the floral business, and Alejandra, employed in the same industry, was able to work from home a few days a week and commute to Chicago the rest. With plenty of land surrounding their farmhouse, Sean decided to put in a small pasture and purchased three cows for the sole purpose of raising them to feed his own family. Soon friends and other family members back in Chicago began placing orders, and, as demand grew, he realized there was quite a market for locally raised beef. To fill the increasing orders, Sean purchased a few more cows and added a couple chickens to the mix – delivering farm fresh eggs, hand washed by Alejandra at their kitchen sink. Because many of their customers were from the Chicago area and didn't have enough freezer space to store half or a quarter of a cow, Sean searched for a butcher who would package the meat into smaller orders. In addition, the butcher had to be USDA certified because legally the product couldn't cross the state line without being processed in a USDA facility.

I found out about the Buchanan-based ranch on Facebook while researching sources for locally grown beef and pork. Multiple friends recommended their products, and I was directed to their website (finnsranch.com) where I was impressed by the variety of products they offer and drawn in by the pictures of the boys feeding the animals. I signed up for the weekly newsletter to receive emails about special offers and updates from the ranch blog. When I asked Sean about how he started to get the word out about his growing business, it turns out early advertising for the ranch was just as grassroots as the farm itself. In the beginning, they printed fliers and gave them to friends to share. In their first year of selling farm-fresh products, they even traveled back home to the South side for the annual Irish Parade where they walked the route and passed out information. They also went to local gyms and fitness centers to promote their homegrown products to the health conscious. Sean was still working full time at his day job, so he was able to slowly build it up during the night or the weekends. All the while, the couple kept buying more chickens and cows (and added pigs as well) and began researching the best types of feeds for the animals. Two years ago, they transitioned from conventional feed to non-GMO feed for the chickens and switched to 100% grass feeding for the cows, another selling point for their product and an advantage over their competitors.

Before long it became apparent that the family would have to decide whether or not to make the ranch more than just a side job. In the winter of 2014, Sean became disillusioned with changes pushed by his employer, and the couple decided to jump into the farm business with both feet. Sean retired from the floral business in January of 2015, right before the busy Valentine's season, and officially became a full-time farmer. To provide for their family after this momentous career change, they started investigating farmer's markets in Chicago to sell their products during the spring and summer months. Today, the markets provide the biggest source of income for Finn's Farm, and they participate in six to seven markets per week. They also started a winter delivery program to sell their product during the cold months. On Wednesdays, Sean loads up his delivery truck with beef, pork, and eggs and drives into Chicago to drop off the orders to 20 locations where it will be purchased and picked up by his customers. To add to their growing list of products, they purchase turkeys to sell in the fall, ducks for their eggs, and contract with a farmer in LaGrange who raises dairy to sell pet milk. They also purchase certified organic vegetables from a local farmer in Three Oaks to offer their customers. Many of their products (vegetables, eggs, and meat) are purchased using a program called Consumer Supported Agriculture. The idea behind a CSA is that customers place a standing order for farm products and pay ahead, helping the farmer buy seed and feed and pay for all the front-end costs that go into producing the product.

The Finns have also started the process to become a certified organic farm, a procedure that involves a lengthy application and site visits by state officials. To have a certified organic pasture, the land must be chemical free for three years. Of the 14 acres of land they own, six of the acres are currently used as pasture, and they are continually taking down more timber to create more pasture. They also lease additional land from Buchanan residents to raise the beef to meet growing demand. There are 17 heads of cattle currently in their home pasture, another three in neighboring pastures, and 12 in Indiana, for a grand total of 32 cows. Sean's goal is to eventually have his own breeding stock of 30 cows producing 30 calves. With help from his boys and his neighbor, Ron, they move the cattle from one side of the pasture to the other whenever the grass supply gets low.

Finn's Ranch is certainly a busy place, and his two young sons complete many of the daily chores.

Nicholas and Matthew oversee feeding and taking care of the chickens, ducks, and pigs and feeding the cows hay during the wintertime. They wake up early in the morning to start their routine, and it continues after they get home from school every afternoon. To provide some context to the scope of this job, the Finns will have 600 chickens laying eggs this summer. In addition, they will purchase 100 additional meat birds from a hatchery in Holland every four weeks and raise them for the eight-week time period of time it takes to have them ready for the butcher.

Sean will tell you that he never intended to quit his day job and become a farmer, that it was a natural progression that just sort of "happened." In fact, he knew very little about farming when he decided to buy that first cow. The ranch is a prime example of "learning by doing," and he credits many fellow farmers and friends he's met along the way, either at the co-op or local farm supply stores, for helping him figure it all out.

He grew up in the city, but made frequent trips to visit his grandparents in northern Wisconsin where he spent a lot of time playing outside and fell in love with the great outdoors. As a teenager, he picked up hunting as a hobby and joined his brother on hunting trips to central Illinois to visit college friends who lived and farmed in the area. The love for the outdoors is what drew him to Coveney Road in Buchanan; in this land he spotted the opportunity to spend his days in the wide-open spaces of the countryside. He laughed as he remembered that when they bought the house, he thought he would, "*maybe buy a couple of chickens and a cow or two.*" That simple plan has grown into a fully functioning farm with plans for expansion, and the city boy from the South Side of Chicago now spends his days moving cattle and repairing fences—and he wouldn't trade it for the world.

The family has folded right into the fabric of their newly adopted hometown, and many friendships with other Buchanan families were formed through summer nights spent at the ballpark and winter days watching floor hockey at the high school gym. Such is life in a small town, where community sports are the central attraction, and connections are formed when cheering for the hometown team.

Our tour ended with a visit to the turkey pen, and I returned to the dining room table to chat with Alejandra. Her warm and engaging nature extended my planned trip from one hour to two, as I found myself completely enthralled by their transformational story. The couple met as professionals in the flower business where she used to sell him carnations. Originally from Colombia, Alejandra moved to the United States with Sean to start their family and says she can live anywhere.

She enjoys the simple pleasures of their new farm life, especially when she can take the time to sip her morning coffee on the back deck and gaze over the green fields that have become her home. Alejandra continues her career as a Buyer for the floral department of a mass-market grocery store company based in Chicago. It's all about teamwork on the farm, and the Finns have organized their busy schedule to make sure someone is always at home when the boys get off of the bus.

The Finn family's passion for this new lifestyle is evident in every aspect of the ranch. The free-range chickens happily roam over the rolling hills, their vibrant feathers adding a touch of color to the otherwise green landscape. Their clucks combine with the crow of the rooster and the quacks of the ducks to provide a continuous barnyard symphony. The fence lines that run the length of the property are well maintained, and the cows they house are bright-eyed and muscular. It is clearly a labor of love and a sight to behold. When asked what he enjoys the most about trading in his business suits for flannel shirts, Sean responded that he loves the daily work involved in maintaining the farm and getting to spend his workdays in the fresh air. I can't say I blame him. Judging by the view from their back deck, it's hard to imagine how the concrete jungle could ever compare with the tree lined paradise of Coveney Road.

# GO NORTH

The distance to Arch Rock is measured in stair steps – 204 to be exact. And my son and daughter ran up most of them in an attempt to be the first to reach the top. With a four and a six-year-old, everything is a competition. The panoramic view of Lake Huron was well worth the sweaty hike, and we even managed to get a picture at the top with two proud kids and a thumb-sucking baby along for the ride. This was just one scenic stop on our eight-mile bike ride around Mackinac Island and one of many mental snapshots that I will assuredly look back on with fondness as my children grow out of the pull behind bike trailer.

North is usually the answer to whatever ails you. Feeling exhausted by the rat race and cooped up in your office? Go north. Feeling too connected to the digital world and out of touch with your primal self? Go north. Kids more concerned with what's happening on YouTube than what's happening out in the woods? Go north.

To be sure, I didn't always feel this way. There was a time when the annual family trip up north was met with a whiny, "*Do I have to?*" During my teenage years I was more concerned with missing out on plans with my friends than I was with packing up the van, hooking up the boat, loading up the tackle box and sleeping bags, and driving to the Upper Peninsula. On my last trip north with my family, before I became old enough to stay home on my own, I detested the idea of spending an entire week fishing. When we arrived at our cabins in Canada, I announced that I was walking into town to meet some people my own age and would be back when I found something else to do.

And that is exactly what I did. Within 15 minutes I'd found a group of teenagers to hang out with for the next seven days. When I foolishly decided to hop in a truck and go to a party with my new gang one night instead of returning to my cabin by curfew, my understandably frantic parents spent hours knocking on doors in town until they found my whereabouts. This was pre-cell phone era and now, as a parent myself, I want to return to that evening in 1995 and smack my thirteen-year-old self for putting my parents through such a frightening search. But, as a thirteen-year-old, it was a pretty cool night. Hanging out in a sauna at a lake house with new friends who ended every other sentence with '*eh* was one for the books. And my parents doled out a fitting punishment: I was forced to spend the entire next day fishing…in a boat…with them.

Looking back on our annual pilgrimages to the North Woods, my mind is flooded with memories that turned into epic stories to later be re-told over campfires throughout the years, each telling more colorful than the last. Like the time we crossed into St. Ignace at the exact moment a classic car parade was making its way down the main street. And how my dad, instead of stopping to let it pass by, drove right into the middle of it with our green Dodge Caravan and old fishing boat. Not one to miss an opportunity to embarrass his young daughters (who were now crouched down in the backseat), my dad rolled down all the windows and waved and honked at the spectators standing on the side of the road. When a man in the crowd yelled out, "*Nice rims*!", we couldn't help but momentarily forget our embarrassment and join our parents in laughter.

When I revisit that simpler time in my mind, I always picture my mom (who during the other 51 weeks of the year wore high heels and dresses to the office) wearing my dad's camouflage hat and tennis shoes, content to spend an entire day on the lake reeling in massive pike and walleye. I can smell the breakfast of eggs and bacon that she cooked on the stove of our camper or the tin foil dinners she made over an open fire. I can see my little sister, ever the woodswoman, exploring in the forest or joining my dad fishing on the dock as I sat at a picnic table reading the latest Nancy Drew mystery or Sweet Valley High saga. I can feel the warmth of my sleeping bag, as I lay awake in the still of the night, listening to the voices of countless aunts and uncles and cousins retell the highlights of the day around the glowing campfire. I can hear the low cry of the loons on the lake, signifying that we were North indeed.

Despite my teenage resistance of the pull of the North, all of the summers spent there must have imprinted themselves on my DNA. Now, as a parent myself, I'm bound to subject my own children to this same fate as well. When my son was eighteen months old, he dipped his chunky little feet into the frigid waters of the rushing Tahquamenon Falls and cried when we took him out of the water. I should've known then that I had myself a Northern boy. Now six, he spent the last week starting his own campfires and baiting his own hook. The image of him at the end of the dock, sitting by himself on top of an overturned five-gallon bucket with his line in the water and the sun setting down over the trees will forever be imprinted on my heart.

I think the Northern bug might've bitten my daughter this week as well. She didn't hesitate to strip down to her underwear and jump into the lake within ten minutes of our arrival to the cabin. Seaweed be darned, the girl was going swimming. Her two cousins, Grace and Tinley, joined her on all her adventures and their collective six hands and feet stayed appropriately dirty all week long. They were watched over by my little brother, a keeper of the fire himself. My sweet baby couldn't resist the lake either. She couldn't have cared less about the little leech that attached itself to her leg during an hour-long romp on the sandy shores. I think she somehow knows that it's a badge of honor, an initiation of sorts to the North Woods and a tale that will be told around future campfires.

So, for a week, all was right in the world. The Wi-Fi was replaced by a connection to the woods. The race to work was replaced by a stroll to the lake. The queen-size pillow top mattresses were replaced by squeaky camp beds shared with a cousin or a Nana. Rushed dinners between sports practices and work meetings were replaced by Uncle Donnie's famous burgers on the charcoal grill and a family of thirteen around a picnic table. Nightly bubble baths in a carpeted bathroom were replaced by camp showers and an aunt-led assembly line of French braids. NickJr shows were replaced by Papa's telling of the Legend of Sleeping Bear Dunes.

Chalk it up to the call of the wild or the call of the loon, the North has a way of getting into your bones. You can breathe a little deeper up there. It is a place where little boys take a step closer to becoming men with each fire they start. It is a place where princesses transform into daring adventurers with dirt under their pink fingernails and leaves in their braids. It is a place where moms and dads become trail guides and lumberjacks and tellers of tales. It is altogether magical and intoxicating. It has the dual power to isolate you from the rest of the world and connect you to what really matters. But be warned, once you sit under the hard pines and soft birch, your soul will never again be able to resist the pull of the North.

# WHO CARES WHAT THEY THINK?

*"You wouldn't care so much about what people thought of you if you knew how seldom they really did."*

Ouch. Those words simultaneously bruised my ego and released me from the pressures of self-consciousness, which is not an easy task when you are a sixteen-year-old girl. When my dad threw those harsh (but true) words of advice out there, in the midst of a drama-laden moment from his teenage daughter, I don't think he realized what a tremendous impact they would have on my life. The moment was, if you'll excuse the cliché, paradigm shifting. But the truth of those words stuck with me over the years. Live your life the way you want to live your life. Do what you want to do, and be what you want to be. Don't worry about what others will think, because they are too busy living their own lives to worry about yours. Basically, the world doesn't revolve around you, kid.

My dad's advice, once I got over the initial sting, was tremendously liberating. Have you ever been self-conscious out on the dance floor? Guess what…so is everybody else out there. The good news is that they are more concerned about how *they* look busting a move than about how *you* look shaking your groove thing. If you want to get on the fast track to conquering your fear of dancing in public, just attend a Zumba class. Most of the women poppin' and lockin' were probably once wallflowers too, before they realized that nobody really cares *how* you look when you dance—only that you showed up to join the party. I can tell you from experience that I am completely oblivious to the movements of my fellow dancers because I am way too intent on following the steps myself. I received further evidence to support this theory when one of the instructors recently yelled out, *"There are no wrong moves….just accidental solos!"* So, dance like no one is watching because, really, no one is.

You can imagine how helpful this piece of advice—that people are too busy living their own lives to worry so much about my daily decisions— can also be for students who are nervous to deliver a speech in front of a classroom full of their peers.

Glossophobia, or the fear of public speaking, is a widely shared condition and one that can be difficult to overcome.  My conversation with students who suffer from this phobia usually goes something like this:

Student: "*I'm just too nervous to talk in front of people.  I think I'll take the point deduction on my grade and just skip the speech part of the assignment.*"

Me: "*Oh, you're nervous to talk in front of the class. I totally get that.  You should volunteer to go first then.*"

Student: "*What?!  Didn't you just hear what I said…I am terrified of public speaking. Why would you tell me to go first?*"

Me: "*Because, if you go first, the only person who is really going to be listening to you is me.  Everyone else is going to be too busy thinking about what they are going to say when it's their turn.  They will be polite and quiet when you are speaking, but they won't really be listening….they will be practicing their own speeches in their own heads. So, basically, you will just be talking to me.*"

Student: "*Really? Nobody cares about what I have*

*to say?"*

Me: *"It's not that they don't care....they just care about what they are going to say more. And the students that aren't stressing about their upcoming turns at the podium will be too busy subversively texting to pay attention to your two-minute lesson on the Mongols."*

Student: *"Oh...well I guess I'll do it then."*

Bubble burst. But, with truth comes confidence. And overcoming a fear of public speaking in front of their own peer group, a crowd of self-consumed 17-year-olds, will hopefully make other obstacles in their lives seem less scary.

These guiding words can be applied to other areas of life as well. Worried about how you look in that dress? Don't be. Every other girl in the room is thinking about how she looks in her own dress to be much concerned about yours. Stressing over changing your major in college? You shouldn't. You're the one who has to take the tests and work in that field; others have their own jobs to trudge to on Monday mornings. Concerned about what other runners will think about your split time for that last mile? Hate to break it to you, but they were too busy looking at their own watches to notice. You know what does matter though? That you put on the dress, that you value education, that you laced up your kicks and got off the couch.

It's easy to get wrapped up into the dueling evils of peer pressure and groupthink. We are bombarded with images of "perfection" every day and encouraged to keep up with the Kardashians. Our society breeds self-doubt and self-consciousness. I know that my own kids will soon enter that dreaded phase of considering others' opinions when making decisions that will only impact themselves. But I hope to buck that trend entirely, or at least keep it at bay for as long as I can. I intend to foster an environment that will encourage my son to bust out his best dance moves to a medley of One Direction songs every year at the elementary school talent show, regardless of the potential for embarrassment. Because what you do becomes who you are. If he repeatedly takes on challenges and isn't afraid to put himself out there, he will grow up to be a man with integrity, a leader who follows his own code of ethics instead of the crowd.

So, make bold choices. Live confidently. Sit in the front row. Dance in public. Take a chance. Go for it, always.

# TAKE A HIKE

There are few problems that can't be solved by a walk in the woods. Feeling stressed out by the daily grind and rundown by the rat race? Throw on your hiking boots, take to the trail, and feel the weight of the world melt away with every step. Have a problem that's weighing on your mind? Nothing a few quiet hours with Mother Nature can't solve—it's amazing the clarity that comes when you can hear yourself think. Have that cooped up feeling that comes from a long winter stuck inside? Replace the four walls of home with a canopy of hardwoods. Simply put, go take a hike.

There is a certain kinship that my family has always shared with the woods. For us, the woods is like another family member, one who is always there to consul and confer, listen and relieve. In fact, when I think of my grandfather, the woods is the first image that comes to mind. He devoted countless hours exploring and explaining the features of the forest to my sister and me. We spent every season of our childhood in nature's classroom: tapping maple trees for syrup in the winter, gathering morel mushrooms in the spring, camping out under the stars in the summer, and hunting squirrels in the fall for his famous soup. He'd make tea out of mulberries, salve out of rosehips, and jam out of wild raspberries. For my grandpa, the woods provided everything he needed in life, without asking for much in return. But he gave back to the woods nonetheless—he gave his time and his energies, his love and respect.

The woods are a place of refuge for many. For my father, the woods provide an escape route from the modern world with all its trappings and demands. A businessman by day, forced to travel to the city and socialize with the suits, he hastens to return to the quiet serenity of the tall oaks by dusk. You can gauge his happiness by his proximity to the shagbark hickory trees that cover his property. He'd much rather mingle with the maples than schmooze with the CEOs. And while it's been his sanctuary for half a century, it's played a much larger role than simply a retreat. Just as the woods provided sustenance for my grandfather, it's also provided a livelihood for my father. When the recession hit hard and my dad had a family to feed and keep warm, he took to the woods for both. Our freezer was always full of deer steaks and our home was always heated by firewood collected and stacked by his own two hands. While the rest of the world is obsessed with Fitbits and iPhones, skinny jeans and ironic T-shirts, my dad still prefers the comforts of wool and flannel accessorized by his trusty splitting maul and a muzzleloader.

Following the family tradition, my little brother also counts the woods as his closest friend. He hasn't attended school on November 15 for as long as I can remember, and he'd much rather spend his Spring Break clearing new trails than lying on a beach. I remember coming home from college and waking up to the sound of his little green frog boots walking across the kitchen floor. I'd open my eyes to catch a glimpse of his diaper as he escaped around the corner and through the back door before dawn, armed with a plastic shotgun and headed for the backyard. I'd watch through the window as he'd crouch behind a tree and await the perfect shot at an unsuspecting squirrel. And now, immersed in his teenage years, he still prefers the view from his tree stand to the lights of the big city. And what's even better is that he frequently allows his little nephew to tag along. Forget the pull of the X-Box and the allure of the iPad, my son gladly leaves them behind every time he has a chance to escape to the timbers. A few weeks ago, he spent an entire Saturday blazing his own trail in his Papa's woods. He is so proud of this new path that he named it Vine Trail, an ode to the plants he had to cut through to clear it. What says seven-year-old boy more than dirty hands and muddy boots earned from a day of work in the wilderness?

Yes, a walk in the woods is good for the soul. Sometimes all a body needs is a bit of fresh air and exercise to clear the cobwebs and reboot the spirit. I felt this regeneration myself last weekend as I took a hike with my family on Easter Sunday. As the cousins raced ahead, each climbing the big hill with their little legs to be the first kid to reach the campfire site, the parents followed behind at a more leisurely pace, one that is not possible in the car-lined streets of the city. And as the generations all reconvened at the top of the hill, we paused for a moment to take in the beauty all around us. Grandbabies watched quietly as a sandhill crane made its majestic descent across the lake below, and they listened intently as their Papa pointed out the different tracks left by the various woodland creatures that had recently visited the site. In that moment I didn't miss a single thing from the modern world.

So, whether you are looking for a place to roam or a place to belong, the woods will provide. Escape the electronics, plug into nature, and trade in your high heels for hiking boots—I promise you'll find a

much stronger connection than any high-speed
cable can offer.

# THANK A FARMER

*"Despite all our accomplishments, we owe our existence to a six-inch layer of topsoil and the fact that it rains."* ~Anonymous

This was the quote that ran through my mind on the drive out to my parent's house this past Sunday afternoon. It was the perfect Midwestern spring day—seventy-five degrees with a light breeze and plenty of sunshine. The kind of day that begs you to jump in the car and take a drive out to the country with the windows rolled down. As the kids and I crossed over the St. Joseph River and took the scenic route to the west side of town, I gazed out at the endless rolling fields and the familiar rows of mounded earth stretching far off into the distance. The comforting smell of freshly tilled soil wafted heavily in the air, and we waved at Mr. Schutze, ambling down the road perched high atop his trusty tractor—the same one that's carried him down countless rows and the last few decades. It's planting season in my little hometown, and this time of year has a way of reminding me just how essential those folks are whose livelihood depends on the soil and the sun, the temperature and the rain.

I grew up in this town, yet my personal farming experience is limited to my failed attempt to plant and tend a garden a few years back (*"Oh, you have to water the plants...like, regularly?"*) and that one time I grew a tomato (yep, just one). Yet, I have always been drawn to the process and revered its practitioners from afar. Farmers hold a place of honor in the legend and lore of pure Americana, and for good reason. What other profession is more responsible for the continuation of the human race than farmers? Despite this position of importance, what other group is more humble in their role than these same men and women who sacrifice sleep for our sustenance and only quit when the job is done? It's kind of hard to punch out when the sun is your timeclock.

The agrarian backbone of our community is tied to every aspect of life here. As children we took field trips to the School Farm, a real-life working farm with animals and crops maintained by a local family who live on site and run by Mr. Mark Nixon, the longtime principal of Moccasin Elementary

School. Every October, the kindergarten classes pick out bright orange pumpkins from a patch planted at the farm, and first graders visit twice a year to learn a lesson about decomposition by burying trash in the fall and digging it back up in the spring. Second graders make homemade apple juice at the farm and each successive grade has its own trip surrounding a special project. In April, the School Farm hosts Old Fashioned Plow Day, a well-attended event for the community that boasts of a pancake breakfast, demonstrations by early tractors and draft horses, a petting zoo exhibit, tractor parade, 4-H projects, sawmill and quilting demonstrations, and hayrides. The sponsors of the event are local families, businesses, and farmers who love to support the preservation of agriculture within our community and our school system.

In the summer we can find a showcase of the fruits of their labor at our growing Farmer's Market located downtown next to the library. It's the main reason I stopped trying to grow my own garden—it is much easier (and tastier) to buy my produce fresh from the source every Saturday. My kids love helping me pick out red potatoes and green beans that are pulled straight from the field, loaded into a truck, and displayed on wooden stands just low enough for their little arms to reach. We round out our shopping trip with a fresh jar of honey, a quart of blueberries, and a loaf of freshly baked apple bread. If I'm feeling generous, I even let the kids pick out a cookie from the church bake sale stand. On our way home we drive out to Red Bud Trail and make a quick stop at Vite's Greenhouse for their famous sweet corn. No summer cookout is complete without it; it's a homegrown treasure that has become a weekly staple on dinner and picnic tables throughout the county. I like to serve it on the side, right next to a juicy grilled pork steak from Strefling Farms. A person could get spoiled with such easy access to all the goodness that comes from our local fields.

But if you want to get a handle on the farm culture during any season, all you have to do is make a visit to the McDonald's in town every weekday morning for the early riser coffee crowd. Rumor has it that the old guard meet up there to talk seeds and weeds and discuss the weather and the state of our world. Man, the collective experience of that group and the stories they could tell. One of these days I'm going to meet them for coffee and ask them the secret to growing a successful tomato plant.

My three little blonde-haired, blue-eyed nieces are growing up as farmer's daughters and living every part of a country song. Their daddy plants and plows for a living and they love visiting him at work where he gets paid to breathe in the fresh air and play in the dirt. Just a little more than a week ago, he and my sister welcomed their third baby girl into the world. The next day, while Mama and Baby Allison were recovering in the hospital, Donnie decided to take the girls to the farm for the day instead of dropping them off at school. That night he posted a picture of the sisters walking side by side out in the field with a big red barn and a split-rail fence in the background with the caption, *"Probably not getting the education they would've gotten if they'd gone to school today, but still learning something nonetheless."* Isn't that the truth—such value to a day spent connecting with the land.

But I guess it doesn't matter if farming is in your blood as long as its roots are in your soil. I can already tell that my own kids have inherited a fondness for farmers. They love watching Farmer Matt bring his big machines out to our field to cut the alfalfa and roll it into giant bales of hay. They sit on the porch and wave to him as he passes by in the hot afternoon, and, in the evening, they gaze out their bedroom windows and watch him load up the last of the bales unto his trailer as the sun sets low over the horizon. *"We sure have a nice view,"* my son will remark as he looks out across the freshly cut field. It's moments like these that I am thankful for the land and the bounties it produces and glad that I made the decision to raise my little ones in the wide-open spaces of farm country where there is always enough room to stretch their legs and always enough dirt to cover their toes. And I'm thankful that Farmer Matt, and the rest of the Warda crew, continue on the traditions of their grandfathers.

In the arena of farming, the few serve the many. So, the next time you run into one of these hardworking folks around town, either searching for a replacement part at the hardware store or driving their John Deere down Front Street, shake their hand or give them a nod and say a simple thanks. And if you see them in a corner booth at Hilltop Café, buy them a cup of coffee or pay for their eggs and bacon. Chances are they're responsible for more than a few breakfasts served on your kitchen table.

# ALL THE WORLD'S A STAGE

I spent the day in a fairytale, surrounded by princesses and peasants and the Big Bad Wolf. The Three Little Pigs were there too, and as they played cards on a blanket on the grass, I snacked on pretzels and grapes with Snow White and Little Red Riding Hood. I discovered the secret to Fairy Godmother's magical powers (a generous dose of glitter powder might be involved) and learned that sometimes a King needs to wear a wig to cover up her blonde ponytail. It was an afternoon of enchantment and theatrics and the good kind of drama. For ninety minutes on a steamy Sunday, a simple stage in my hometown was transformed into a far-away kingdom and a talented group of kids transported us to a world of make-believe.

For the last month, my two oldest kids and my niece practiced with a crew of local thespians to put on a rousing performance of "Beauty Is a Beast" and other "Fairytales with a Twist" at The Tin Shop Theatre in Buchanan. Under the guidance of Director Kelly Carlin (Aunt Kelly to my kids) and Stage Manager Megan Goodrich, thirty kids ranging in age from 4 to 20 were coached and corralled into an impressive cast list bursting with enthusiasm and talent. Have you ever hosted a kid birthday party and attempted to direct the group of invited youngsters in the playing of an organized game or a coordinated activity? Now imagine doing that every night for a month. Throw in wardrobe changes, memorized lines, and a packed audience, and you will get some sense of the enormity of their task. Forget the pretend magic playing out on stage, the real wizardry takes place behind the curtain by two ladies dressed in black and whispering instructions to adolescent actors waiting in the wings.

It's a pretty amazing thing to see your kid on a stage, illuminated by the spotlight and pretending to be somebody else. Logically you know this is the child you tuck into bed every night, but every few minutes you catch yourself believing that this character is authentic, and this storyline is real. It's a transformative experience for them too. My sweet little niece Gracie, often shy in real life, took the stage every night with poise and confidence and impressed all of us with her natural acting abilities. Typically the last to volunteer, she was the first to raise her hand to try out during auditions and the concept of stage fright doesn't appear to be on her radar. My son, an actor since birth, has found an even larger stage than his YouTube channel provides and relishes the feedback from the audience. And my daughter, a five-year-old fashionista, well she finally found an acceptable excuse to wear makeup. Watching her backstage as the older girls apply mascara to her baby lashes and lipstick to her pursed lips, I'm thankful she is growing up surrounded by accomplished young ladies who demonstrate character and radiate talent. They are all experiencing a sense of camaraderie that is so special for children their age, and I am forever grateful for the older kids who have taken my three under their wings.

And speaking of the older kids, I'm not even sure how to express my wide range of amazement for their abilities. These are teenagers who willingly put on wigs and ridiculous costumes and walk out on stage in front of family and friends and, more importantly, other kids their own age. Conventional wisdom would suggest that kids in this age group would rather walk off a cliff than risk an embarrassing incident in front of their peers, however, these kids aren't your typical teens. They are self-assured and brave, feeding on the palpable support of their cast members and fueled by the electricity of a performance under the lights. They fight back the nerves and step out onto the stage, knowing the experience is worth the anxiety. It is encouraging to see so much raw talent concentrated into one group of kids and refreshing to see how humbly and graciously they accept their nightly accolades. They are the leaders of our next generation, the ones who will put in the work and get the job done. The ones who will take risks for new discoveries and encourage others to do the same. I'm confident that their futures will hold many more performances deserving of our applause.

So, as they say in theatre, "*That's a wrap!*" (I'm a stage mom now, so I know all about theatre lingo.) But the friendships gained during the many hours of rehearsal and the lessons learned over the course of six performances will continue long after the last guest has left the playhouse. More importantly, this experience has left me with a profound sense of urgency for the support of the performing arts for youth in our area. Budget cuts and decreased funding have crippled the abilities of school districts across the nation to provide such opportunities for their students. It is now common to see theatre classes squeezed out of the curriculum and drama departments dropped entirely. Administrators who would love to offer a wide array of performing arts programs find their hands tied by a national education movement more concerned with STEM courses (Science,

Technology, Engineering, and Math) than a well-rounded student. Our schools, and our students, are suffering from a lack of enrichment opportunities. It is up to us, the parents and the business owners and the community at large, to cultivate and encourage a community that values the performing arts. It is our responsibility to support the amazing programs that already exist in our schools (both with our dollars and our attendance) and cheer on the efforts of community members who provide similar after-school opportunities for our kids. So, as a parent and a community member, I would like to say a huge thank you to the people who work behind the scenes to provide our kids with experiences in the fields of performing arts and music and theatre and stage production. The leaders of our fine arts programs, the companion of performing arts, deserve our appreciation and recognition as well. In a world filled with harsh realities and devastating news headlines, we should all work together to support the sanctity and beauty that an art-enriched life can provide for our children and encourage them to jump into a fairytale and escape to a faraway land of make-believe, if only for a few hours.

# THE MAN, THE MYTH, THE MUSTACHE

*"Mornin' Miss Dodson."*

I haven't responded to this title in years, but for this person, I happily reply, *"Good morning Mr. Mucha."*

You see, Mr. Mucha was my teacher, my siblings' teacher, my parents' teacher, and basically everyone else under the age of 55 who lives in our little close-knit community. And if Mr. Mucha wants to call me by my maiden name, well then that's just the way it's going to be.

I still remember my first day in his class. I was a freshman and feeling a little like the first refrain of Taylor's Swift song "15." As roll was called and friends responded with either the obligatory "here" or a smart-aleck response in the hopes of eliciting a chuckle from the peanut gallery, he got to the Ds, and paused.  The conversation went something like this:

Mucha: "*Another Dodson, huh?  Are you related to John Dodson?*"

Me: "*Yes, he's my uncle.*"

Mucha: "*I'll have to keep my eye on you.  He was the only guy I knew that had a back-up cheat sheet for his cheat sheet.  What's he doing these days?*"

Me: "*He's a lawyer.*"

Mucha: "*Well, I'll be damned.*"

And from that very moment, I became a fan. I joined the masses in hanging out by his classroom between bells, repeating Mucha-isms, and hoping that he would throw a wisecrack in my direction. Isn't that funny?  We wanted him to make fun of us--because it was always out of love, always in a light-hearted manner, and always hilarious. And, if you were lucky, he made up a name to call you that would stick with you for the rest of your four years there, if not the rest of your life. Just ask my buddies Jack and Slick Nick.

Mucha is old-school; it's part of his charm. If you were late to class, he wouldn't assign you a detention or send you to the office or even record it on your attendance record. Instead, he'd make you do pushups. While explaining the morning board work to the rest of the class, he'd throw a little line of encouragement to the tardy student - "*I might not be able to make you smarter, but I can make you stronger.*"

If you grew up in our small town, chances are at some point Mr. Mucha was your coach. He led every team under the sun--from football to women's soccer to little league baseball. The only sport he didn't coach is lacrosse, and that's only because we don't have that here. But I'm sure if you'd told him you wanted to start a lacrosse team and needed a coach, he would've said, "*Sure, why not? Now go find some of those little sticks with the nets on them and I'll meet you down at the field.*" And, if he wasn't your coach, he was probably calling the strikes behind the plate as an umpire, announcing your name while running the scoreboard, or cheering you on from the stands in his characteristically gruff roar. (Admit it, you just did your best Mucha impression in your mind after reading that.)

Every time I get together with old buddies from high school, the talk inevitably turns to tales from our glory days. We talk about that time they cancelled the Homecoming Powder Puff game (the traditional girls vs. girls football game) because of the weather and, instead of going home, we lined the park across the field with our cars, turned the headlights on, and played in the rain. Or the time that we had a plan to T.P. our friend's house and were surprised by an ambush of teenage boys hiding in the trees with Supersoakers. Eventually though, without fail, one of us will start a story with, *"Remember that one time in Mucha's class when...."* and the tale that will follow will elicit howls of laughter. That familiar refrain will be followed by another – starting a chain of knee-slapping and tear-generating stories of our time in his class. There is a special place in our hearts for these stories. His classroom was a safe haven during our teenage years, and each memory transports us back to a simpler time. I can almost smell the coffee and chalk dust just thinking about it.

Lest you think that Mucha could only be counted on for an off-color joke or a lesson on swinging the bat, let me share with you his most valuable asset--his heart. When tragedy strikes a small town, the reverberations have a way of impacting everyone. Unfortunately, we've endured our fair share of heartbreak and loss as a community in recent years. When such devastation occured, we turned to a source of comfort, and that source was Mr. Mucha. Three years ago, we lost a charismatic and beloved young man in a tragic accident that took him from us way too soon. As the heartbroken community mourned this unthinkable loss, we gathered at the football field to seek solace from each other and provide comfort to his grief-stricken family. And then we sat and listened as Mr. Mucha, microphone in hand, pacing the track, delivered the most beautiful, off-the-cuff, from-the-heart message I've ever heard. In that moment, he was the only one who had the capacity and the gravity to speak in a way that both comforted and lectured a stadium filled with teenagers forced to face the reality of their own mortality. And they listened, we all listened, because he was our coach, he was our mentor, he was our leader, and he was our friend.

And as our fearless leader faced his greatest challenge yet in the game of life, I was reminded of all the lessons he taught me since that fall day in 1994 as I sat in his class, gazing out the windows overlooking the football field. He taught me how to do a real push up, not the girly kind. He taught me how to play Euchre (okay, he didn't teach me, but he let me play it in his class if I finished all of my homework). In an effort of epic proportions and against all odds, he taught me math. He taught me that if you want students to respect you as a teacher, then you must first show them you care about them as a person. He taught me that it's not always easy to do the right thing, but it's always worth it. He taught me if you really want to make an impact in a kid's life, you have to be a part of their life.

So here is my small attempt to thank him for his impact. For the way he guided a community and generations of Bucks. For the way he let my six-year-old son join in on the wrestling camp with the big kids, causing him to board the Mucha fanwagon just like the rest of us. For holding my baby when I brought her to school events, even though she pulled at his trademark mustache. For attending the funerals of my grandparents and recalling a personal story about each of them. For every small act of kindness, such as opening the windows of my classroom and turning on my fans early in the morning before the students arrived in an attempt to alleviate the suffocating heat of an early fall day in our non-air-conditioned school. For every grand act of love, such as raising amazing kids of his own who possess his same selflessness and commitment to community.

Thanks, Coach Mucha – for making us stronger and smarter. We owe you a mountain of gratitude. There isn't enough coffee in this world to repay you.

# UNDER THE FRIDAY NIGHT LIGHTS

*"I'll meet you on the hill!"*

We shouted this to our friends as we
temporarily parted ways after school on Friday
afternoons in the fall, only to be reunited a few
hours later at Memorial Field where the town would
gather to watch our Boys of Fall in the hometown
football game. The hill was the gathering place –
close enough to the parents sitting in the stands, yet
far enough out of the way to offer a small taste of
freedom. It was steep—you could roll down it at a
pretty good clip if you started at the top. But you
could also spread a blanket out on the ground and
chat with your girlfriends. If you were the social
type, you could stroll around to see who else was
hanging out. The flat area at the top was the perfect
width for a pick-up football game between middle

school boys who dreamed of one day wearing the maroon and white jerseys and playing under the lights themselves.

When you grow up in a town of 5,000 people, social life revolves around the high school athletic calendar. Not much has changed since the autumn days of my youth. Friday nights in September and October are still reserved for football games at Memorial Field. The kids who used to roll down the hill are now the parents sitting in the stands, occasionally glancing over to check on their own little ones. That's the thing about a small town—the more things change, the more they stay the same. There is a comfort in that though. It is satisfying to know that you can leave town for ten years and then show up at the field on a brisk Friday night and spend the next three hours cheering for the home team and catching up with your old principal, your old flame, your old buddies, and everyone else in between. And when you finally do manage to sit down in the stands, you make a beeline for your family's "spot." You know you'll find them there, cheering on the home team just like they have been for the last thirty years. Small town folks are creatures of habit.

Three generations of my family make the top left corner their own. This is the spot where my grandpa sat to yell for my Dad and his buddies on the field back in the late 70s. It is the place where my mom sat to cheer for that same guy, her high school sweetheart. This corner has played host to an endless supply of aunts and uncles, cousins and friends, all here to hoot and holler for whatever kin of ours was out on the turf for the night. It is from these bleachers that my parents watched me jump and fly down on the track with a cute bow in my ponytail, singing out the lyrics to the fight song. They even got to leave those seats one half time in 1997 to escort me down the field as Homecoming Queen. And now I return to this corner, to cheer on my students on the field while keeping an eye on my own Little Bucks rolling down the hill.

It's funny, really, how many lessons and stories from my life have Memorial Field as the backdrop. Every time I stand and place my hand over my heart during the National Anthem, I think of that hill. I think of the time I was running around with girlfriends and the announcement came on to *"Please rise for the playing of our National Anthem."* I think of how we didn't stop and didn't rise and continued to run and giggle during the first few bars. I remember my dad sternly calling out my name and motioning me over to him with a look in his eyes that was reserved for only the worst offenses. I will never forget the words he said to me through clenched teeth:

*"Do you see that flag right there? That is a flag*

*that many men—your own grandfathers and uncles—have fought to honor and sacrificed their lives to defend. That flag represents freedom. That flag is the symbol for the greatest country in the world. When the anthem is played, you'd better stand and look at that flag. And when you look at it, I want you to think about all the people who have fought to protect our country and keep us safe. I better never see you talking during that song again.*" Message received. And a good one it was.

It is at Memorial Field that I learned another lesson—to work hard for a lofty pursuit. A group of 15 friends popped enough popcorn in the concession stand to pay our way on a school trip to Washington, D.C. A trip that would inspire me to return to that city years later to work and live for a season—a country mouse in the big city.

I'm sure many others can trace lessons and stories back to this sacred ground. With charismatic coaches pacing the sidelines and colorful announcers in the press box, there has always been quite the cast of characters to offer up lessons on camaraderie, loyalty, and heart. Coaching legends such as Karpinski, Pops, and Mucha are household names in our hometown and sure to come up in discussion at post-game celebrations or high school reunions. I always love listening to my dad and his buddies tell old football stories with these guys as recurring characters.

That is the power of a football coach. They send boys into battle every Friday night, and it's their job to arm them with enough toughness and heart to make it through. The best ones inspire boys to be men and farm kids to be kings of the field. And we, the spectators, get to watch it all play out. We get to cheer on our warriors as they plunge headfirst into 300 pounds of opposing muscle. We get to hold our breaths as these boys of 16 and 17 crash into each other, helmet-to-helmet, in pursuit of seven points and screaming fans. And, in this ever-softening world of hurt feelings and wimpy resolve, it is refreshing to watch some good-old-fashioned smash-mouth football—if only for a few hours.

The current coach, Reid McBeth, will surely find his own way on that list of legends in the years to come. He is leading this current crop of Bucks to a series of victories, each one more impressive than the last. The boys who currently don the maroon helmets with the big "B" on the side are a living testament to the hundreds of men who came before them. Every time they throw on their jerseys, every time they make their way down the long stairs, cleats clicking on the cement, they play for an entire town and a way of life. They are our gladiators— our keepers of the good old days.

So, if you ever find yourself in our neck of the woods on a crisp Friday night in the fall, look for the lights of Memorial Field and follow the throngs of adoring fans dressed in the colors of the Buchanan Bucks. Come and feast on a dinner of hot dogs and popcorn, and enjoy the sounds of our small but mighty band.  Walk on the bricks of our main entrance, engraved with the names of alumni and teachers, coaches and fans. For good luck, touch the sign honoring our #88, a gladiator who played with a full heart both on and off the field. Take in the sights and sounds of a small-town Friday night in all of its glory.

I'll meet you on the hill.

# HAIR COLOR AND HOMECOMING

I left two cans of temporary hair color on the kitchen counter along with a note: "*The pink one is for sister and the green one is for brother*." Two hours later, a young man walked into my classroom wearing a full orange tuxedo complete with a ruffle undershirt and orange top hat 'a la Dumb and Dumber. The very next hour, my communications class serenaded the English teacher with a choreographed lip sync ensemble of a Bruno Mars hit. Yesterday a young lady covered her arms, face, and legs with white and blue polka dots using window paints while another teacher wore plaid shoes with a tie-dyed shirt and striped pants. And on Monday, students flipped their clothes around and walked backwards to class. This could only mean one thing. It's Homecoming Week in my hometown.

Like many small towns across America, excitement here comes in the form of community events. When you have four stoplights, you don't get many requests from rock stars begging to hold concerts at your stadium. You also don't get famous authors holding book signings, red carpet premiers, or museum galas. But you do get Homecoming—a real-life, honest-to-goodness, celebration of fun and high-school-reunion all rolled up into one.

It all starts on Monday when every kid from pre-school to 12th grade dresses up for the first of five themed days decided by the high school Student Council and celebrated district wide. We've had some real doozies lately. For example, a few years ago we decided to have "Duct Tape Day." Do you know how many patterns and colors of duct tape are available? Chevrons and animal prints and camouflage, oh my! Kids who hadn't raised a pencil to take a single note since the beginning of the year stayed up all night to create one-of-a-kind duct tape ensembles. Who says kids aren't engaged in the educational process these days? The cleanup of discarded silver accessories at the end of the day was well worth the laughs produced during the seven hours of sticky madness. Some kids had a harder time "disrobing" than others…it all depended on whether they had applied the tape to cloth before putting it on or decided to forgo a protective barrier altogether. Again, still worth it.

Another one of my favorite days from the past was "Fake an Injury" Day. Oh, the creativity! The hallways looked like a hospital ward. I haven't seen that many bandages since the last episode of M.A.S.H. The smart ones milked their faux injuries and explained that they couldn't take tests (sprained writing hand) and couldn't run the mile warm up for gym class (on crutches due to a fractured knee). One kid even created his own doctor's note excusing him from all educational tasks and homework for the day—too strenuous, just recovering from pretend gallbladder surgery.

But Homecoming isn't all about dress up days. That's just the beginning. The week is filled with float building and class competitions. The other sports teams—volleyball, tennis, and soccer—host their own home games and add to the buzz of school spirit in the air. The anticipation builds with each day, growing to a crescendo on Friday.

Starting around 9:00 a.m., the senior athletes, cheerleaders, student council and pep band make their way to the elementary and middle school buildings for the annual Traveling Pep Rally. The little kids get to meet the big kids (the REAL rock stars in their eyes) and get to experience what it means to be a part of The Herd. In our community, school pride is cultivated from the very beginning. The band snakes through the hallways, and students join in line as the drum core passes their classrooms. When everyone is finally situated in the gymnasium, the spirit team leads the students in raucous cheers and the fight song and the cheerleaders twist and turn in the air to the "oohs" and "aahs" of the impressed audience. When the mascot finally makes an entrance, he or she is greeted by hundreds of screaming little Bucks—a scene reminiscent of 1964 Beatlemania. I'd be lying if I said Bucky hasn't been knocked to the ground a time or two by a rushing crowd of adoring kindergartners anxious to pet his hair and give him a high five.

After the traveling pep rally, the busload of kids perform an impromptu "parade" on the sidewalks of the main street downtown. Cars honk and folks emerge out of downtown offices and stores to wave and clap along. This is all a precursor, of course, to the high school pep rally that takes place during the last hour of the school day. As with everything else related to school spirit, we like to go all out for this one. Our Master of Ceremony (who doubles as the gym teacher) likes to make an entrance. And let's just say he isn't above using fog machines and strobe lighting for effect. His costume borders on the absurd (in the best way) and continues to build on the year before, getting more outlandish every year. I can neither confirm nor deny if his plans for this Friday include real deer antlers. He comes from a long line of over-the-top M.C.s, however. A few years ago, our co-hosts descended down the football stadium steps perched atop inflatable pool rafts that were carried by the football team in a manner similar to the Egyptian Pharaohs. Too much? Never.

And after the last human pyramid collapses to the ground and the individual winners for the days of the week are sashed, hordes of fourteen to eighteen-year-olds are released for the afternoon with the instructions to meet back up in a few hours for the parade. I bet you've already guessed that every school kid in every grade has a float they belong to. These homemade floats are paraded through town and end up at the stadium, with enough candy to fill the Titanic thrown to the crowd along the way. Chances are you are either riding in the parade or sitting in a lawn chair, watching someone you know pass by. It's kind of a big deal.

Around 7:00, the main event kicks off, and the next three hours are spent cheering on the team, eating salty popcorn, watching the half-time show, and talking with friends you haven't seen in years. That's what happens at a small-town Homecoming game—people actually come back home, if only for a night. For three hours, the most important team in the world is wearing maroon and white and you hold your breath every time the ball is launched into the air. Between plays, the men standing along the top of the stadium reminisce about games that were

played on this same field over twenty years ago—
games they can still feel in their bones. Every pass
is remembered, every tackle recalled. And now,
they watch their own boys out there, and their eyes
beam with pride.

The women—mothers and aunts and
grandmothers— sit in the stands and cheer for their
babies on the field or along the track. Their claps
muffled by warm gloves; they will yell out phrases
they learned from years spent on aluminum
bleachers. Every so often, their minds will play
tricks on them and the muscular seventeen-year-
olds with the numbers on their backs will transform
before their eyes into rocket football players with
too big pads and grass-stained knees. Their hearts
will ache for those long-ago days, and they will
wish for the time on the scoreboard of life to just
slow down a bit.

And when the last second has ticked off the
clock, the crowd will stand as one and sing the fight
song, joined by the gladiators of the field, helmets
held high. The throngs of fans will depart through
the stadium gates and go on to celebrate another
victory in the books. Many will head downtown to
toast old friendships and tell old stories. Kids,
who've been allowed to stay up long past their
bedtimes, will be carried from cars to beds with
sugar still on their teeth and grass stains still on
their knees. The Homecoming Queen will place her

crown on top of her dresser and admire the shine still emanating from the best night of her life. The town will retire to their homes and tuck away another small-town memory.

It's just a whole lot of fun. There's no other way to describe it. For one week out of the year, kids get to be kids, and we all get to remember what it's like to have fun. In a world dominated by high stakes testing and the Common Core, it feels good to let kids dye their hair green and wear silly outfits to school. Deadlines get pushed aside by duct tape and bubble sheets are replaced by polka dots. And those big kids, the ones who grew up and left town years ago, they get to trade in their business suits for sweatshirts and come back home, too.

# A PLAN AND A PURPOSE

He walked onto the court with a plan and a purpose. The plan was written on a piece of paper, first folded long ways and then folded again in half and tucked into his three-quarter sock or his waist band.  Every practice, every game, he had a plan.  It served as his road map to success:  focused practices led to wins, wins led to the playoffs, and the playoffs ended with a State Championship.  But the plan was just a vehicle for a larger purpose. A purpose that was more significant than any trophy, more valuable than proper layup form, and far more crucial than the number of tallies in the wins column. The purpose would serve his girls long after they'd hung up their basketball shoes and scored their last three-pointer.

The purpose was simple: Believe—in your abilities, in your value, in your team, in yourself.

Twenty-five years ago Coach Bill Weaver led the Lady Bucks Basketball Team to the Class C

State Championship and brought a proud community along for the ride. This was such a momentous event that former player Kelley (Prosser) McNamara fondly remembers, *"coming back to town with a police escort after the championship game and seeing people come out onto the streets to cheer and welcome us home brought tears to my eyes."* This significant achievement was the crowning jewel of an impressive thirty-year career spent as a teacher, coach, and mentor in the little town of Buchanan. Another player, Shelley (Colpetzer) Kilgore, can still remember the look on his face after they won the state championship and described it as *"priceless and proud."*

From 1979-2009, Coach Weaver lived and breathed basketball and his infectious love for the game inspired a generation of Bucks to fall in love with it, too. If you graduated from Buchanan during that time, chances are you were fortunate enough to cross his path at some point. He was your gym teacher, your coach, your Junior Bucks Basketball coordinator, and your summer camp director.

It's not like you could really miss him: his height gave him a towering presence and his booming voice echoed from the gym and permeated the hallways of the school. He was everywhere— dressed in his signature warm-ups, a whistle on a lanyard around his neck, a basketball tucked under his arm, and a smile so welcoming that even the most complacent teenager couldn't resist. And that laugh—so hearty and contagious that it made you want to be a part of whatever was causing it just so you could hear it again. Letitia (Bowen) McGuff, a member of the 1990 State Championship Team, remembered, "*We were so serious and disciplined in practice that when he laughed, we usually didn't expect it, and it allowed all of us to recognize and be reminded that our hard work was such fun!*"

On the court, Weaver was focused and intense. When asked to recall her favorite memory of her coach, Belinda (Deeds) Thompson said, "*Although I like to tease him about it, my favorite memory is him pulling me off the bench by my ponytail to get me to the check-in table when he wanted me back in a game.*" His old-school toughness and strict discipline paired with an open and giving heart earned him the highest level of respect from players, parents, and officials. But despite his numerous awards and accolades (and the list is long), Coach Weaver always remained humble. His players recall that he never liked the attention that was directed his way and always chose to deflect praise to his team. According to Thompson, "*He didn't share the spotlight: he instead redirected it to shine fully on those around him.*"

Coach Weaver preached sportsmanship before it was cool. He stressed the importance of representing your school and your community in a positive way, both on and off the court. This lesson even found its way on to the playlist of pre-game songs during his tenure. Many of his players remember bursting out of the locker room when the first lines of *Be True To Your School* by the Beach Boys rang out over the gym's loudspeaker. Carrie (Flenar) Franklin recalled that sportsmanship was as important to Coach Weaver as winning. According to Franklin, "*He taught it, modeled it, stressed it and expected it daily. We didn't argue calls, we didn't taunt opponents, we didn't play dirty, and we weren't arrogant. He wouldn't stand for it, and we knew it. We respected the game, each other, our coaches, the fans, the officials, and our opponents. We learned that it was equally important to handle both wins and losses gracefully.*"

Coach Weaver never missed an opportunity to demonstrate his love and devotion to his kids. Lesley Shepherdson's favorite memory of her coach was the attention he paid to the little details of life from the "special water" he brought to practice every day, to the small gifts that he gave to each of his players. Although I never played basketball, as one of his students I will never forget his attention to the small things. On my first day as a sixth grader in his gym class, he asked all of us to share our birthdays. When I said that my birthday was June 22, he flashed his brilliant white smile and let out a gargantuan chuckle before revealing that he too shared his birthdate with me. He then said, "*Birthday buddy, I'm going to call you Junebug.*" And every summer, for many years after our first encounter, I would receive a birthday card in the mail addressed to Junebug with a gift card to Pizza Hut or a kind word from my birthday buddy. He recognized what many do not—that the small things are often the big things.

He cultivated teamwork and harped on the importance of attitude. Hope (McBeth) Dryden remembers his commitment to the concept of teamwork and said, "*From the top of the line up to the bottom, he made us all feel like we were special and an important part of the team.*" When his former players were asked to recall their favorite memories of their beloved coach, without exception every single one of them mentioned the "WE WILL" statements. The "WE WILLS" were a list of twelve affirmations created by Coach Weaver that outlined how the team would practice, play, study, work together, grow as a team, and succeed. They were memorized and recited by the players before every practice and every game. The statements were framed on bedroom walls and scribbled in notebooks. They became so ingrained in each of his players' lives that all admit to still utilizing them as adults. Katie (Carpentier) Shelton said, *"His "WE WILLS" became fundamental to our daily routine as a team, and later to my own basketball teams. We will have positive attitudes has become paramount in my classroom where I frequently remind my students to "choose their attitude*!" Jennifer Prosser unequivocally stated, *"Everything I learned about goal setting, I learned from Mr. Weaver."* Nicole (Smith) Spencer added, *"As I coach my own basketball team now, I often catch myself thinking what would Mr. Weaver do?"*

Perhaps his greatest asset was his availability to his players off the court. He was a staple at graduation parties, attended countless weddings, and kept tabs on his players long after they'd left the hallowed halls of BHS. He spent countless hours opening the gym for extra time to shoot and made sure that every kid that played on his team knew they were valued. Julie (Metzger) Georgeoff recalled how he had a "*special quality in making every one of us feel as we were one of his own, not just another one of his players.*"

How was he able to commit so much of his time to his players and foster personal and treasured relationships with each and every one of them? This question appears to have only one answer— Pam. The fatherly role played by Coach Weaver was rivaled only by the motherly figure that his wife, Pam Weaver, demonstrated throughout his teaching and coaching career. Katie (Young) Sherwood described her as "*The Sunshine of the Team*." Pam hosted team dinners, washed uniforms, and sat behind the bench for every game. She was a constant source of support for the girls and Lesley Shepherdson said of Pam, "*She had a way of always putting everyone first with her unconditional grace and caring ways. There were times after a mistake on the court and I would come to the bench, it was just her sweet smile of reassurance that would let me know my mistakes were okay and I would do better next time.*" Their combined dedication made them an unbeatable team and a powerful partnership to have in your corner. Kaycee (Pritchard) Wagley reminisced about their role in her life and said, "*Mr. Weaver was more than just a coach, he taught me more than the game of basketball. He taught me about the game of life. When I hurt my knee and had surgery, it meant the world to me that Mr. and Mrs. Weaver would take me to physical therapy and coach me through the hardest physical challenge of my life.*"

But in coaching, success lies in the final score, the total wins and accumulation of titles. Weaver's numbers don't lie—his methods worked, and he has the record to prove it. He holds the Women's Varsity Basketball coaching record of 340-132 with an amazing .720 winning percentage. His overall coaching record was 439-221, an astounding .665

winning percentage. His teams racked up nine conference championships, seven district championships, two regional championships, and one state championship. He was named the 1990 Basketball Coaches Association of Michigan Coach of the Year and I don't even have enough space to mention the rest of his awards and accolades.

But his impressive record only tells part of the story. It doesn't tell how he took a group of individuals and turned them into a team. It doesn't show how he mentored an entire generation of kids and instilled values that would serve them long after the final seconds ticked off the scoreboard. The numbers prove that his plan worked, but they don't reflect his greatest purpose: to encourage kids to believe in their worth and believe in themselves. No, you can't measure that in winning percentages or engrave that on a plaque. This purpose was too big to be tucked away in dusty old scrapbooks and too important to be relegated to distant memories of pep rallies and police escorts. It is a legacy that lives on in the hearts of his former players and the pride of a small town.

So, as his former players gather at the home basketball game this upcoming Friday night to honor Coach Weaver's legacy and celebrate the 25th anniversary of the State Championship, he will assuredly try to turn the attention to his girls. He will probably talk about their importance in his life and will certainly downplay his role in the whole affair. He might not even remember the small details and the big life lessons that he imparted on all of us.

But WE WILL.

# THE REAL HEROES OF YOUTH SPORTS

*"Every little boy just wants to be a hero."*

This theory has driven my dad's coaching philosophy for more than 30 years of leading youth sports teams. I learned of this simple maxim during a conversation we had years ago regarding my little brother's hockey team—a group of boys who, under the guidance of my dad, managed to go five seasons without a single loss. It wasn't because they had superior talent (although they were pretty darn good), and it wasn't because my dad pushed them to the limit and demanded excellence (although he's been known to run a pretty hard practice), it was because he understood that all kids crave greatness and he consciously put them into situations in which they could become heroes. He'd send them out onto the court (or the field or the rink) with a pep talk for confidence and a slap on the helmet for courage. And after they'd scored the go ahead run or the winning goal, he'd welcome them back to the sidelines with an enthusiastic "*Atta Baby!*" and a big ole' bear hug. And after each game, the boys seemed to walk a bit taller and stick their chests out a bit farther. Pride feels good to a kid.

It takes a special person to make a second grade soccer game feel like the World Cup, but a great coach knows that spirit and grit can take a team farther than talent alone ever can. Great youth coaches inspire confidence and can turn a rag-tag team of country boys into a fine-tuned victory machine. They can transform a group of small-town volleyball players into a cohesive record-breaking unit that believes they are worthy of winning. And sometimes, they do much more than that.

I remember my dad driving around town for an hour after every rocket football practice, the back of his truck loaded down with ten-year-old boys in shoulder pads, to drop off the kids whose parents never came to pick them up. I remember one of his players sleeping on our couch for a few months because his mom wasn't around, and he didn't have a place to stay. Luckily, my dad isn't the exception to the rule. Many youth coaches take on much more than the responsibility of teaching kids how to catch a ground ball or how to throw a perfect spiral. Whether it's giving a kid a few bucks for lunch money or checking in with them to make sure their homework is done, coaches regularly take time out of their own lives to provide a safe place to land or a shoulder to lean on. Just last week one of my high school students gave a speech about the most influential person in his life. In his speech he talked about a guy who treated him like a son on and off the field, who inspired him to be a better man, who led by example, who exuded strength and kindness, and a guy who he wished he could be like someday. This seventeen-year-old kid was talking about his assistant football coach and there was no mistaking the importance of his influence. Kids crave acceptance and love, and the best coaches offer an abundance of both.

We've all seen the sports movies that follow the same predictable plot line: coach takes on team of misfits, coach inspires team to believe in themselves, team takes on a competitor that is bigger and better, team relies on lessons taught by coach, team wins, and coach looks on with pride in his eyes as his misfits are transformed into champions. There is a reason why we pay good money to sit in a crowded theater to watch these movies. We've all had one of those coaches. We've all been part of something greater than ourselves. We've all had our day in the sun. And if we haven't, then we'd sure like to. Because pride feels good…but knowing that someone is proud of you feels even better.

So, thank you to all of the coaches out there who race from the office to the court every night of the week. To those who miss meals with their families to make sure one of their players makes it home safely. To those who give up overtime at work for quality time on the field, and trade quiet nights at home for raucous nights in gymnasiums. To the men and women who volunteer their expertise and their guidance, their time and their love. Thank you for treating our kids like your kids and creating situations in which they can become heroes.

# HOCKEY TRADITION RUNS DEEP

We don't really care that you don't "get it." It doesn't bother us that you find the whole concept silly. Yes, we know we can't play it past 8th grade and we understand it won't earn us a college scholarship. It doesn't change our complete devotion and utter obsession. We can't help it; it's in our bones. Our parents played it and we played it and now our kids play it. To be honest, you'll never get it, unless you grew up here. It's an exclusive club with generations of members. You have to be a native to appreciate its pull. You have to be a Buck to understand floor hockey.

I walked into the high school gym this past Saturday to join the rest of my community in celebrating the opening weekend of floor hockey season. For those unaccustomed to the sport, it is hockey played in tennis shoes on a gym floor with hard plastic sticks, bright orange pucks, and hundreds of screaming fans. The arena is made up of homemade plywood boards, lovingly assembled every Friday night by coaches with power drills and disassembled and stored away every Saturday afternoon after the games. In our town, floor hockey has achieved cult status and throngs of adoring spectators and decades of former players flock to the stands every Saturday in January and February to cheer on this year's new crop of players. If you grew up in Buchanan, chances are you played floor hockey every winter from 1st through 8th grade. It's likely that you can still remember your coach, still recite all the players on your team's roster, and still recall a few prized match ups from the good old days. It's not uncommon to reminisce about championship floor hockey games during high school reunions, reliving each pass off of the boards and each 'flicked' puck in the net.

Buchanan is a working-class town. It's not the kind of town where residents use their expendable income to purchase expensive ice time at a rink or buy $200 Bauer skates. And there is a certain sense of pride that we're not like the "rich kids" up the road—we cherish our role as small town country kids. But it is a town in love with the idea of hockey. So, back in the 70s, some of its residents organized a floor hockey league for the kids in the community. My dad was among the first group of players in that inaugural season, along with his friend Kimi Klug. They were both on the first all-star team that traveled to Battle Creek, a huge deal back then, to play against teams from Canada and other Michigan towns in an international tournament that continues today. Since then, they've both coached their daughters, son, and now grandchildren in countless winning seasons. They hold "Godfather" status in the hockey family—along with others like Wayne Writer and Grandpa Jack Hemminger.

My first memories of floor hockey involve tagging along with my dad to practice and playing with the older boys. As a young punk coach for his even younger brothers Randy and Dan, he had a chip on his shoulder and a penchant for winning. He devised plays—affectionately known as "Three Across" and "Three Up and Down"—and used phrases such as "No Man's Land" to describe the area in front of the goalie. I'll never forget watching the last game of my Uncle Dan's 8th grade season from high in the stands of the high school competition gym (in the days before we switched to the auxiliary gym). He played with guys like Robert Hickok, Ian Hall and Jimmy Mosier, boys who would grow up to coach their own kids and run the hockey program themselves. The boys of Team Moose #449 (local businesses sponsored the teams both then and now) in their aqua blue t-shirts won a hard fought battle against their best friends on the other team and secured an undefeated season in the last floor hockey game of their life—and then we all went to Pizza Hut to celebrate. It was epic as only a small-town sports event can be.

Fast forward a few years and it was my turn to take the court. Almost from the beginning, my dad decided to make me a goalie. But not just any goalie—he decided I was going to be a "stand-up" goalie, something rarely seen in floor hockey. The vast majority of floor hockey goalies play on their knees in the net and only use their stick to block incoming pucks. But stand-up goalies, well they act just like ice hockey goalies and can run out into the court and use their stick to hit the puck to the other side of the court. I even scored a few goals of my own using this technique. Every night during hockey season, my dad, sister, and I would make our way down into our basement for shooting practice. I would tuck my long french braid under my custom painted goalie mask and my kid sister would take 100 shots on me from various positions, and I would have to block them all. As you can imagine, by the time it was her turn to play, she was already an Ace with a wicked backhand. These basement practices were not unique to our household. Throughout our town, cement floors on the lower level were turned into hockey courts complete with nets and taped lines on the floor.

Lanny Fisher, all-star player and now a long-time coach, hosted countless basement hockey games in his childhood home where neighborhood kids would gather on cold January nights to defend their honor and practice their moves. Did I mention we are a town obsessed?

When I played in the 90s, the biggest event of the year was the All-Star trip to Canada. Every year, a team of 12 girls and a team of 12 boys were picked from the house leagues to represent Buchanan in an international floor hockey tournament in Windsor, Canada. We would practice for weeks and leave school early on a Friday to ride for hours in a yellow school bus to our tournament destination with our parents following behind us in a long caravan. To say it was a huge deal would be an understatement. To the kids on that team, it was everything and countless tales of bravery played out on those hardwood floors. We played with friends we would later win high school championships with in high school sports. Coached by my dad, Mr. Aalfs, Mr. Bagwell and Mr. Sunday, the teams of my middle school days were filled with athletes such as Jamie Johnson, Jenny Wesner, Kelly Enright, Courtney Huebner, Niki Heller, Jenny Mosier, Dawn Brown, Krystal Carpenter, Sarah Wiggins, Sarah Taylor, Sarah Bagwell, Sarah Durren, Megan Leinonen, Carrie Aalfs, Jessica Walkden, Stacy Kubal, Katie Martin, Mary

Glossinger, sisters Kary and Kacy Couchman, Tori and Kimi Aalfs and Julie and Lisa Sunday. The boys team of the mid-90s was made up of guys like J.R. Rauch, Troy Paskiet, Nick Powers, Teh'Ron Guidry, Ricky Pickens, Jeff Miller, Derek Dreitzler, Jacob Labounty, Jeff Berry, Bryan Lloyd, all of the Baker Boys and many, many others.

We came dressed in our old sweatpants and our maroon t-shirts to play against teams wearing matching warm-ups and shiny black helmets. We faced off against Forest Glade and Scarborough, Recognition and Lansing. Our parents hated their parents and, true to hockey tradition, more than a few skirmishes started by sons on the court were later finished by fathers in the parking lot. Our moms and grandmas yelled from the stands and lived up to the true meaning of "hockey moms." It was tough, it was gritty, it involved a whole lot of trash talk, and we loved it. And after the games ended for the day, the Buchanan teams retreated to the hotel for an evening spent at the pool. For many of our families, the expense of a hotel room for two nights was a luxury and required a sacrificial cut in the grocery bill for the next week. I can still picture all of our parents hanging out by the pool, relaxing with coolers of beverages and take-out pizza, and talking about the time that they faced off against teams from Freemont and Battle Creek.

Our travel teams were fierce and scrappy and desperately wanted the championship trophy and one year we finally managed to bring it home escorted into town by the local fire department and police force (sirens blaring) and interviewed by the local news channel.

Years later, somebody came up with the ingenious idea to host our very own hockey tournament in our own gym. To this day, teams from around the state travel to little ole Buchanan and live out their glory days just like their mothers and fathers before them. My sister, with a quick shot and an even quicker temper, took her turn playing in the family tradition in the 2000s alongside the little brothers and sisters of the kids I played with—players like Jackie Mosier, Val Klug, Libby Glossinger, Ashley Warda, Nicole Tucker, Ashley Carpenter, Michelle Johnson, and all three of the Bender girls (Lauren, Shelly, and Ali). Guys like Matt Warda, Nick Gowan, Brad Huebner, Jason Stroud, Chris Mondschein, Stephen Mitchell, and Tim Weber carried on the torch for the guys before them. Many of these former players now coach or watch their own kids play. My sister Caryn watches her daughter Grace run around on the same court she used to play on, blonde ponytail bopping around just like her mama's used to do.

To say it is a family affair for most of Buchanan would be an understatement. If you played, so did your cousins and you were probably coached by your aunt or your uncle. I can't even count all my cousins who played through the years. Players like Chrissy, Keriann and T.J. Sears (coached by Uncle Randy Sears), Josh, Jake, and Jordan Wahlstrom (coached by Uncle Scott Wahlstrom), Jacklynn and Alex Leiter, and Perry and Makinzy Wahlstrom (coached by Uncle Perry Wahlstrom), Jenna and Tanner Phillips (coached by Uncle Ted Phillips), and Andrea and Grant Hemminger (coached by Uncle Chris Hemminger) were just a few of the kin who suited up every Saturday.

Just last year my little brother Brendan finished his last floor hockey game and ended the season with another undefeated record and a citywide championship. My brother was basically born with a hockey stick in his hand and doubled up with floor hockey and ice hockey games every weekend for years. My dad retired as a coach after my brother's last game, ending a 30+ year coaching career and happy to now sit in the stands and watch as his own kids coach. Well, to be honest, he doesn't actually sit in the stands. Every Saturday morning in the winter you can find him standing alongside the boards, yelling at his grandkids to "J it up!" or "Swing!" or "Board It!"—old habits die hard.

When my kids stayed the night at my parents last night and discovered, for the first time, the bin of hockey trophies and medals in the basement, they demanded to get them out and display them on the shelves. They can't wait to win their own trophies and score their own winning goals. They look forward to playing in city tournaments and swimming in hotel pools. Just yesterday my son Cy scored his first goal in his very first floor hockey game. This wasn't his first goal ever…he's been playing ice hockey for two years now and has his fair share of hat tricks. But it was his first floor hockey goal and, in Buchanan, that's a rite of passage. And there are more of them coming through. In two short years my fierce little red-haired beauty will get her chance to take the floor. She's already playing ice hockey, but she lives for the day she will get to play in our hometown gym. She will be followed by her little cousin Tinley and her baby sister Kaliana; each one feistier than the next with decades of hockey blood coursing through their veins. They will play alongside the kids of my former teammates and a tradition will continue for another generation.

So, do you see why we get upset when out-of-towners try to tell us it's not "real" hockey? Because to us it isn't just a game. It is a tradition, a multi-generational story, a tie that binds us to our fathers and our brothers, our sisters and our kids. It is a language that only we speak and a history that only we understand. And I dare anyone to ever try to take it away from us. They would have to pry our yellow and red hockey sticks ringed with black electrical tape from our cold, dead hands. Too much? Sorry, we hockey families tend to get a little carried away. I'll take a two-minute penalty for roughing and see you back on the court next Saturday.

# FOR THE LOVE OF THE GAME

Have you ever seen someone fall in love? Ever witnessed the transformation that takes place as their actions are led by what their heart wants? The object of their obsession becomes all they can think about, all they can talk about. Their days revolve around this new love and every waking moment is devoted to nurturing this special connection. It is both instant and all consuming. Although I didn't see it coming, I sure couldn't miss it when it happened—this summer, as I sat watching from the bleachers, my son fell in love with America's pastime.

Like any true love, it was instant and intense. As he climbed into the backseat of my van after his very first practice, I immediately noticed something different about his eyes. In them I saw passion and excitement, giddiness and bliss. I casually asked, *"So, how'd you like it?"* His response was immediate, and I knew right then and there that a fire had started in his soul on that warm May evening at the dusty little league park. He looked at me through the rearview mirror with sparkling blue eyes peeking out from underneath a too-big ball cap and replied, "*Mom, I love baseball.*"

I have to admit, I was a bit surprised. In all our focus on ice hockey over the past three years, we'd neglected to spend much time outside throwing the baseball around. Our evenings were spent at the ice rink, not at the ballpark. Our basement was full of sticks and pucks, not bats and mitts. To be honest, when I sent him out there for his first practice that night, I was a bit worried that his lack of skills and experience in this sport would make him hesitant to get out there and play. But he was undeterred by the steep learning curve ahead of him. Love is blind, and he saw only the possibilities and none of the pitfalls. It didn't matter to him that a simple game of catch turned into a round of "chase the ball down." He didn't care that most of his throws hit the ground before they hit his partner's mitt. And although he didn't know where to stand when playing second base before practice started, he was a self-described expert in field positions by the time it ended. I admired his blind allegiance to his newly discovered passion. He reminded me of the boy in the song, "*The Greatest*" by Kenny Rogers, the one who swings and misses three times and marvels at his own pitching skills as opposed to focusing on his strike out.

As his passion grew, so did his ability. The kid who couldn't catch a cold in May became the starting second baseman in June. The boy who missed every pitch at the batting cage in pre-season became the leadoff batter and a reliable base runner by game time. This wasn't from dumb luck or pure natural talent; he just worked hard at getting better. Every night after dinner he grabbed his mitt and bat and headed outside for an hour or two of practice. He played whenever and wherever and became an expert at begging any nearby adult to just, "*Pitch him a few.*"

I couldn't help but fall in love right along with him. His excitement was infectious, and I found myself holding my breath every time he stepped up to the plate, willing him to get a hit just so I could see the smile on his face as he hustled down to first. I noticed other Moms and Dads in the stands doing the same thing, cheering on their little guys and yelling things like, "*Get your hands back*" or "*Keep your glove down.*" Over the course of the season, the families on the sidelines merged into a cohesive tribe of enthusiasts, calling out the names of the boys in the blue jerseys and relishing the big hits and the clutch plays.

Our evenings were spent at the corner of Liberty and Carroll Streets, on the same diamond generations of Buchanan boys spent their summers. Across the field we could hear the Girls of Summer banging out doubles and running around the bases. Those tough softball chicks with their long ponytails sticking out from their helmets and their black eye paint were the sisters of the boys on the grass covered infield and many families stood between the two fields to watch both. All of us ballpark parents fed our kids hotdogs and nachos for dinner followed by more suckers than we're willing to admit. Younger siblings were free to run around with the other kid sisters and little brothers whose summer schedules were also dictated by the game calendar. We became part of the community of the league where every other night was a high school reunion. It was like stepping into a time machine and setting the clock back twenty years, except this time the faces that filled the field during my youth were now the coaches standing on the third base line and the moms cheering in the stands. The continuation of a tradition is one of the beautiful aspects of small-town life, made even sweeter by the successive generations that wear the jerseys and come back to watch their children and grandchildren do the same.

There are all kinds of lessons to be learned on the field that can translate to lessons in real life. To keep swinging, even with two strikes against you. To win humbly and lose gracefully. To play a role for the good of the team and to cheer on your teammates, even if from the bench. To learn from a missed ground ball and keep your head up and your mitt down for your next chance to come along. To never give up--some rallies begin with two outs on the scoreboard. To experience the elation of winning and the agony of defeat. To play with your heart and leave it all on the field.

Yes, summertime is for ball. It is for friendly rivalries and good old-fashioned competition. It is for nail-bitters that come down to the last pitch of the last inning. It is for muggy evenings and rain delays, dirty faces and grass-stained knees. It is for coaches who believe in their players and lift them up after a hard loss and celebrate with them after a big win. It is for slushies and hot pretzels, bubble gum and walking tacos. It is for rally caps and bows made of yellow leather. It is for rundowns between second and third and slides into home. It is for homerun derbies and little league records, championships and trophies. But most of all, it is for holding on to a little piece of Americana and a continuation of the love of the game.

# THE MAN WITH THE MUG

Softball is a warm weather sport. It is a sport
of farmer tans, sunburned ears, and sweaty helmets.
It is a sport that necessitates sliding shorts; a
protective barrier for the thighs of players who
would rather risk cuts and bruises the size of a
dinner plate than wear polyester pants in 90-degree
weather. It is a sport that requires a dugout—a
shelter offering a half inning refuge from the
sunbaked field. It is a sport of orange Gatorade jugs
filled to the top with icy refreshments to quench the
thirst of dusty faced athletes. Yet, when I think of
softball, I think of a mug of hot coffee held by a
first base coach in long pants and a ball cap.

Coach Leon Bagwell waved hundreds of
players down to first base during his thirty-year
tenure as Assistant Coach of the Buchanan High
School Softball program. I'm not sure there has
ever been a better-suited person to grace that chalk-
lined zone. His gruff voice was the first one you'd

hear as you entered the batter's box. He'd call out, "Come on good hitter!" as you dug in your cleats and readied your grip. Verbal courage from your biggest fan. And after you executed the bunt or smacked a line drive over the shortstop's head, there was no one prouder of your accomplishment than him.

I remember the look on his face the day that I hit my first (and only) homerun. I raced down to first base as fast as I could, pumped up by adrenaline and intoxicated by the feel of the bat on the best hit of my life. As I approached first, he greeted me with a fatherly smile and these words – "Slow down Dot…enjoy this one." Sage advice for a young kid. To this day, I can't get through that memory with dry eyes.

Coach Bagwell had a certain charm to him. You wanted to be in his presence because he made you feel safe and loved and confident. But you also wanted to be close to him in the chance that he might utter one of his famous one-liners. My all-time favorite was "Lord love a duck!" This expression was reserved for moments of exasperation—a frequent occurrence when coaching teenage girls. It would come on the heels of a missed call or a base running error. It wasn't a put down and it wasn't necessarily directed at any specific player. It was just a way of recognizing the mistake and then moving on. It always reminded me of that famous scene in A League of Their Own when a shaking coach Jimmy Dugan, played by Tom Hanks, tries to reprimand an outfielder for missing the cut-off man (again) without yelling at her. Only the best coaches can alert you to your mistakes without crushing your spirit or bruising your ego. Only Coach Bagwell could do it while making you laugh at the same time.

Coach Bagwell was dedicated. He must've hit hundreds of thousands of fly balls over the years as the outfielders coach. Wonder why he needed that mug of coffee? It was probably because he had just finished working a 12-hour shift before the game. Despite this rigorous schedule, he never once complained about sacrificing sleep for softball.

Another coach in the same program, Rachel Carlson, recently recounted her favorite Coach Bagwell story to me. She said that after a 2005 loss to Lawrence at the Bronson tournament, Coach Bagwell was so distraught that he didn't stop commenting about the loss for weeks. After the Buchanan Bucks won Districts and Regionals, the team took a long trip to Grand Rapids to play Galesburg-Augusta in the state quarterfinal game. Galesburg was heavily favored, and the Bucks beat them in a thrilling 2-1 final. The team celebrated the entire bus ride home and, as they entered town following a police escort, Coach Bagwell stood up on the bus and said to the cheering girls, "Aren't you glad Lawrence wasn't here today!"

One of his recent players, Brittany Schmidt, recalled her favorite story of her favorite coach. She said that the team was driving to a tournament and had to split up into two school vans. Everyone wanted to ride with Coach Bagwell because he drove the speed limit and let the girls listen to the radio. She was in Coach Bagwell's van, and he merged on the highway using his turn signal. For the next eight miles he got progressively more perturbed as the van kept making a "dinging noise" that he couldn't figure out how to turn off. He kept telling the girls that there was something wrong with the van and that it was driving him crazy. Then they got a phone call from the other van, informing them that their turn signal had been on for the last eight miles. Brittany said that he laughed the remainder of the ride about it. That was Coach-- always the first to laugh, even at his own expense.

There are countless other Coach Bagwell stories told by hundreds of girls who've worn the pinstriped uniform of the Lady Bucks. Most of them involve humor, but all of them recall his pride for his team and his love for his girls. We felt like his daughters because that is how he treated us. And he had quite a bit of practice in doing so, given that he coached his own two daughters, Robyn and Sarah, as well. His fatherly presence on the ball field was enhanced by his wife's motherly presence in the stands. Sandy Bagwell continued to support her husband and "her girls" long after her own daughters graduated and left the team. As he cheered you on from first, she cheered you on from the bleachers…a station she continues to occupy.

I suppose this is the type of support that a small-town breeds. You treat your players like your own daughters because they are the same girls who grew up having sleepovers at your house. You encourage with kindness because you have a vested interest in the success of your players beyond the field. You coach players who, twenty years later, cheer on their own maroon-clad daughters as they smack a base hit and join you at first.

I was thinking of Coach Bagwell lately as I exchanged comments with his daughter Sarah (a classmate, teammate, and childhood friend of mine) on Facebook. I was thinking about how he spent his entire life parenting and coaching girls. He and Sandy were blessed with two wonderful daughters and then further blessed with three beautiful granddaughters (Kendra, Kaitlyn, and Hannah). In the coming months, a grandson will be added to the Bagwell roster. Sarah and her husband Jesse are expecting a boy soon, and I bet Coach Bagwell picked them out a good hitter up there. He's probably rocking Noah in Heaven right now, feeding him one-liners and teaching him the steal sign. I bet he's already hit him a few buckets of fungo. He's assuredly placed his worn U of M hat on his little head, ensuring that his love for the maize and blue continues in his bloodline. And when Noah arrives, he might have the faintest smell of coffee on his newborn skin...a sign that Papa Bagwell held him close and then sent him home.

# A LETTER TO MY ATHLETE

Dear Athlete,

Tonight I watched as you walked into the locker room like you have a hundred times before, head held high and bursting with pre-game excitement. Despite the nagging cough, courtesy of a weeklong bout with bronchitis, you took off your tennis shoes and began the ritual of putting on your gear. You strapped on your protective armor and secured your striped socks with lucky tape, one ring around the top and another around the bottom, just like you saw the older boys do at camp last summer. You threw the jersey on over your pads and slipped on your gloves while I tightened up the laces of your skates. And before you got up from the locker room bench, you paused for a few seconds out of habit to let me repeat the same four words I've said to you from the moment you started playing—"Skate hard out there." And then you grabbed your stick and headed out onto the ice.

You're pretty tough for a seven year old.

As I look at you out there, your name and favorite number emblazoned across your back, I can't help but be overcome by an intense feeling of pride. This emotion is not a reflection of your ability, nor is it attached to your performance. (Although you've had many moments of glory when my shouts from the stands could be heard across the arena.) Rather, my love towards you—my boy in the helmet and hockey socks—comes from an admiration of your dedication at such a young age. You sit in a classroom for seven hours a day and spend your nights at the rink. You finish your homework in the car and eat your dinner on the run. You give up screen time for speed drills and sacrifice free time for ice time. While I consider it an achievement if I make it to my exercise class two mornings a week, you spend most of your evenings throughout the year wearing a jersey.

Sometimes, like tonight, you pair the jersey with gloves and skates. In warmer times of the year, it's worn in combination with a ball cap and cleats. In the spring you wear it over a light sweatshirt (at my insistence) to keep out the cold of early morning soccer games. And this fall you've already asked if you can wear a maroon jersey over shoulder pads, hoping that I will sign you up for your first year of rocket football. You watched this year as our hometown high school team made it to the playoffs this year and you can't wait to run out under the Friday night lights someday yourself.

And I know that we sacrifice a few of the pleasures of life that a more open schedule would allow. We don't eat dinner around the table every night. Sometimes homework and projects are finished at later hours than they should be. You've even missed a few birthday parties and sleepovers in order to keep your commitment to the team or ensure a good night's rest before a big game. But I like to think we make up for our losses by the values and experiences that we gain by being involved in sports. Some of my favorite conversations have taken place in our van on the way home from a game, with you in the back rattling on about your day in between swigs of blue Gatorade. And forget relying on a school-mandated program for physical activity, you burn off plenty of calories running around the bases and dribbling the ball down the field all year long. And let's not forget the friendships we've formed with other sports families and your teammates along the way. There's a special bond that is formed between mothers who share the highs and lows of a season from the vantage point of the bleachers.

I hope that your time on the field (or the court or the rink) is teaching you things that you couldn't learn by sitting on the couch at home. I hope your muscles are growing stronger and your mind is too. I hope while you are scoring goals you are also conquering doubts and building up confidence. I hope you are listening to the men and women who sacrifice their time to develop your skills as well as your character. I hope many of your teammates will become your brothers, and a handful of coaches will become your heroes. I hope you will continue to love the game—because competition will drive you to be better, endurance will push you to persevere, and that feeling of pride and accomplishment will last far beyond the championship game.

I want you to know that there have been moments throughout your life that have caused my heart to swell so full of love for you that it felt like it was going to burst right out of my chest. Your little face as a baby as you drifted off to sleep in my arms, mouth slightly parted and cheeks warm and rosy. The look of excitement in your eyes when you discovered how to navigate your first shaky steps. Your flawless martial arts routine that you paired with an original freestyle hip-hop dance for your very first talent show performance in front of a packed crowd. The sight of you reading a book about fairies to your little sisters, cuddled up on either side of you on the couch and hanging on to your every word. These are all pictures that I will keep in the scrapbook of my mind forever. And the image of you out there tonight, admiring the well-earned medal placed around your neck by your coach…that one is right up there with the rest.

And one more thing, a confession really. Whenever I snap the strap on your helmet, I always sneak a glance at your sweet face—the one with the cheeks that I've kissed a million times. The face that keeps changing, little by little, with every new season. In case you didn't already know, I'm proud of the boy with the clear eyes and the full heart who can't wait to glide out onto the ice and chase after the puck. I'm in love with the young man who puts most of his gear on by himself now and carries his own bag to the car. Thanks for pausing to let me whisper those four words to you through the cage of your helmet and for giving a little wave when you find me in the stands. I'll be in the same spot as always, on your side forever.

Love,

Your Biggest Fan

# SISTER SABOTAGE

We call her Sister Sabotage—and for good reason.

My oldest daughter (and also my middle child) is the ultimate "seize the moment" kind of gal. Unfortunately for my son, her Carpe Diem outlook usually comes at his expense. She relishes in the opportunity to embarrass him in front of his friends. She lives to undercut his impassioned and frequently embellished stories with a dose of harsh reality. She never misses a chance to show him up or call him out. She is the epitome of a kid sister. Poor guy, after dropping hundreds of pennies into wishing wells over the last six years in a fervent attempt to get a brother, he is stuck with two girls— a dimpled disruptor and her smiley sidekick.

It all started a few years back, when she was two and he was four. Ever the performer, he was excited to show off his new Tae kwon do moves in front of a crowd of family members gathered for a birthday party. We all watched and clapped as he moved effortlessly through his routine, landing sidekicks and low blocks like a pro. After demonstrating a strong front snap kick, he stood with his legs shoulder width apart for his final stance. His face beamed with pride. We were so busy clapping and complimenting his skills that we failed to notice his ponytailed sibling make her way from the audience to center stage. Not to be outdone, she decided to land her own front kick. Let's just say, he started wearing an athletic cup after that.

Her desire to steal his thunder continued into her third year. During a highly coordinated Scavenger/Easter Egg Hunt designed by her Nana, she waited for the perfect moment to pounce. This moment came after he had spent fifteen minutes painstakingly sounding out and reading each and every clue left for him. As he read the last clue aloud, the one detailing the location of his hidden basket, she must have sensed that it was written as a rhyming poem. Before he could say the last word, she chimed in to take all the glory by loudly proclaiming, "*It's in the boat! It's in the boat!*" and took off down the hill to confirm her suspicions. Thank goodness he is faster than her, because I never would've heard the end of it had she made it to that basket first. Sister Sabotage strikes again.

There is a reason why he reacted with a disapproving sigh when I mentioned that she would be joining us for his kindergarten class Valentine's Day party last year. True to form, she delivered the embarrassment he feared in her signature fashion. As he was talking with his buddies, she chimed in to inform the group that her brother really didn't have a girlfriend even though he claimed that he did. She went on to explain to the group that, A. she had just talked to his "girlfriend", and she said that they were just friends, and B. *"Mom said that you're not old enough and can't even have a girlfriend until you're in high school."* Satisfied with her daily dose of truth telling, she popped a heart shaped cookie into her mouth, sat back in her chair, and looked at me as if to say, *"Don't worry Mom, I set the record straight."* The look he shot me was a bit less satisfied. Mortified is the word that comes to mind.

I would like to tell you that these are isolated incidents. However, I have a litany of examples to back up the assignment of her nickname. These examples are starting to come more frequently the older, and more competitive, they get. If he is being scolded for not listening to directions the first time, she will interject with a phrase like, *"But, am I being a good listener, Mommy?"* (This query will usually be accompanied by an impish grin and a few bats of her eyelashes.) If he forgot to take his plate to the sink after dinner, and I beckon him from the kitchen to get off the couch and finish cleaning up after himself, she will sidle up to me at the dishwasher and calmly ask, "*Don't you like how I always put my plate on the counter, Mama?*" Oh, sister.

Her most recent foray into the realm of subversion happened today. Her brother purchased a few paintings at a garage sale with his own money, and soon after found a buyer in which to resell them to in order to turn a profit. The buyer (his uncle) indicated that the purchase of the paintings was contingent upon my son cleaning the glass frames before pick up. During his clean up job, he accidentally sprayed the glass cleaner too close to the frame and a puddle of solution stained the mat. He was devastated and on pins and needles for the next hour, hoping against hope that it would dry up and he could close the sale. Luckily it did, and he informed the buyer that he could pick up the paintings—and none would be the wiser. That is, until my lovely daughter took it upon herself to spill the beans (in the interest of full disclosure of course). You know when she starts a sentence with the phrase, "*Well, actually…*" that you are about to feel the wheels of the proverbial bus roll over your back as she throws you underneath it.

I shouldn't make it seem like she saves all of her truth telling for her older brother. She likes to spread the sabotage around. She has no problem announcing that I've worn the same outfit too many times when we are out in public. And don't even ask her opinion on your latest culinary creation if you don't want to know the truth. She has no filter. She has no patience for dishonesty. And she can't stand coming in second place. Combine all of this with the fact that she doesn't possess an inside voice, and you have the makings of many embarrassing moments. But when you hear her laugh—a deep, infectious belly chortle—that usually accompanies these moments of subversion; you will understand why we treasure the moments when Sister Sabotage appears. She is unabashedly daring. She keeps us on our toes and keeps us laughing. I can't help but sit back and admire her colorful narration of daily life as she fulfills her role of Commentator in Chief. And I do sit back. I don't want her to throw a zinger my way.

I have a sneaking suspicion that Sister Sabotage might have some competition waiting in the wings though. Her baby sidekick appears to enjoy subterfuge as much as her big sis. This apprentice can crash through a building block fortress and destroy a Lego town faster than you can say, "*No baby!*" She's already found the power button on the Xbox and utilizes her stealth crawl to turn it off at the most inopportune times for her big brother. Her favorite activity is to crawl up on the fireplace hearth while looking back at me to get a worried reaction. She loves when I rush over to scoop her up moments before a headfirst dive off the couch or seconds before a tumble down the stairs. I see many gray hairs in my future. With their powers combined, they are going to be a daring duo. Watch out world—Sister Sabotage and Babyzilla are on the loose. I've already picked out their matching capes.

# MOONSHINE AND MOONBEAMS

*"Have you ever tried on your Mom's high heeled shoes?"*

*"No. I have my own high heels."*

Such is the tenor of the discussion between my daughter and her dance instructor. Four is the new 14.

This is the same daughter who I found hiding in the pantry eating the jelly beans that I told her (three times) that she could not have before dinner. And the same one who recently asked me, *"Are you really going to wear that to my school? Didn't you wear that the last time you helped out in class?"* The one who melts her father's heart mid-scolding by cooing, *"Daddy, you have such beautiful eyes."* And, yes, the same one who will not be rushed into putting on her socks. Come what may, the seam line will be straight across her toes, or we will just have to be late to story time at the library.

It is a curious and wonderful and maddening thing raising a daughter who has her own ideas about everything. There is a fine line between cute "*I can do it myself*" stubbornness and "*I'm not eating that*" rebellion. Now I adore Alice Paul as much as the next gal, but when my daughter acts as though she is an Iron Jawed Angel after a 50-minute standoff at the dinner table, this mom has had enough. But when I yell out, "*It's broccoli, not suffrage for goodness sake*," she just continues to glare at her plate with the same level of tenacity. She knows that she will lose this battle, but much like her mother, her inner-Xena just can't seem to give up the fight. Maybe, just maybe, with enough willfulness and grit, tonight will be the night that she can achieve dessert status without finishing up the green stuff first. I feel her pain. Stubbornness is a powerful force and runs deep through our matriarchal line. I'll let you in on a little secret though -- I want her to keep fighting. As much as I am exhausted by our 10-round bouts, she is going to need that skill when navigating the world outside of our cozy home.

Sometimes I try to rationalize her strong will. "*She gets it honestly*," I tell myself through gritted teeth. My great-grandmother Elvie used to run moonshine during prohibition. She was the lookout for my great-grandfather who, legend has it, made the best moonshine in the whole county. While he would stir his famous concoction in an old bathtub out in the middle of the back woods in Arkansas, she would stand out on the road and whistle if she saw any lights. Once a week, she would bottle it into two big jars, pack the jars in a suitcase and walk to the bus stop. The bus driver would always ask, "*Elvie, what do you have in that suitcase woman*?" (Side note: she was 85 pounds soaking wet and the suitcase probably weighed half that much.) To which she would sweetly reply, "*Moonshin*e." He would laugh at such a silly notion, and she would get on the bus and make her weekly stop to the police station to sell the best moonshine in the county to the local sheriff. You don't get much tougher than that.

But how do you encourage feistiness while at the same time discourage reckless abandonment? I want my daughter to take a solo trip to Europe in her 20s to visit all the gothic cathedrals that she's read about in her college world history course. I do not want my daughter to take a trip to Vegas on her 18th birthday to visit a little white chapel with a cute boy in a fast car. See my conundrum? How do you temper the fire without snuffing it out completely? It is a delicate balance with girls.

I want to raise strong women. I want them to raise their voices, raise objections, and raise their own stubborn baby girls someday. I just don't want them to do it without thinking about why they are doing it first. I pray that their DNA contains even the tiniest bit of calm-headedness from somewhere along the line. While I'm pretty sure my oldest daughter is a shiny red apple sitting right underneath my tree, the jury is still out on the baby.

I own this shirt that says, "*Well behaved women rarely make history*." I love that shirt. I want my daughters to love that shirt. But I also want them to listen to their teachers, and be respectful to their elders, and show deference when it is appropriate. Long story short – I want them to follow the mantra painted in the locker room of the Dylan Panthers – "*Clear Eyes, Full Hearts, Can't Lose*." Because kind hearts are just as important as strong minds. Level heads are just as important as unbridled passions. Tender hands are just as important as strong fists. There is a time for both, I just pray that they will know the difference.

So, as I'm tucking my sweet girls in tonight and kissing their beautiful little foreheads, I will say a silent thank you to all of the fearless women who've fought mightily over the ages to blaze a trail for my two girls to reach heights unimagined for women of my grandmother's generation. And as my oldest whispers to me before drifting off into a dreamland filled with moonbeams, rainbows, and unicorns, "*I love you so much mom, but I don't miss you at all when I am at sleepovers*" - I will only allow myself one brief pang of sorrow, because a girl who conquers sleepovers today will be a woman who conquers the world tomorrow.

# GIRLFRIENDS

*"We are witches, and this is our secret potion that will turn the boys into frogs."*

This was the explanation I received from five tutu-clad girls gathered around a cup full of leaves, grass and sticks. It was their first chat about boys and, true to their age, the discussion centered on a plan involving teamwork, trickery, and girl power. Action was needed to rid these yucky boys from the playground area, and it was going to take a combination of magic and make-believe. And what a potion they concocted! I just hope this boy-repellant can be canned and stored in the pantry because I might need to bring it out again during the high school years.

The importance of girlfriends cannot be overstated. They are essential in every phase of a woman's life from grade school to nursing home.

They are our secret keepers and our sisters by choice, our confidants and our caretakers. They listen to our rants, share in our stories, and encourage our wild side. They make this ride through life a little easier, a little sweeter, and a lot more fun.

My first best friend was also my first enemy. Niki and I attended rival elementary schools and only knew of each other through the trail of gossip, a road frequently traveled by nine-year-old girls. We shared a mutual affection for the same boy— and this fact alone was enough to stir up a strong dislike, dare I say hatred, for my archrival. The summer before fifth grade, my parents moved us out of the country and into a neighborhood populated by school age kids. Within weeks, I'd set up my first lemonade stand and was posed to rake in the profits I was sure to generate with such a fine location. And guess who arrived as my first customer? Turns out my nemesis lived four houses down from mine. Talk about bad luck. And here she was, showing up on her bike to scope out my new business and probably steal my clients. With a scoff, I welcomed her by sharing my observation that the zipper on her jean shorts was down. *"That'll show her,"* I thought with a good measure of self-satisfaction. With a shrug, she zipped them up and asked if I wanted to go ride bikes. And just like that, we transformed bad blood into best buds. By that afternoon we had traversed the neighborhood, created a secret fort in the woods behind our houses, raided her mom's well stocked pantry for oatmeal cream pies and Captain Crunch cereal, and made a pinky promise to never like that boy again—a pledge we both honored for the rest of our time in school. Sisters before misters, right?! Niki and I were inseparable for the next ten years and became the kind of friends who were allowed to have sleepovers on school nights. We shared many firsts together—first ear piercing (her mom owned a salon and Niki knew how to work the piercing gun…we figured it was better to ask forgiveness than permission that day), first cigarette (two puffs and then we shamefully dug a hole and hid it in my backyard), and first fender bender (apparently we thought it took both of us to change the radio station and that the car would just steer itself). We also shared closets, hairstyles, and a childhood—and developed a bond that has endured to this day. This last summer we sat together in the stands and watched as our two girls played on the same ball team. With any luck, they will find their own share of double trouble as they grow up (minus the danger and cigarettes, of course).

In high school I teamed up with a gem of a girl who eventually became my college roommate. Conventional wisdom advises against sharing an apartment with your high school friend, but our shared living quarters brought us closer and allowed us to appreciate our similarities (we've both been known to snort when we laugh) and our differences (she can cook). There is an old saying that there are two types of friends: the kind that will help you move, and the kind that will help you move a body. The latter is the type of friend I have in Emily. (Don't worry, we only sing about burying no-good husbands in our classic Dixie Chicks karaoke duet - we don't intend to test that theory.) She is the one who drove two hours to wash my hair after a surgery that required my head to be bandaged, and the one who drove three hours to hold each of my newborn children. It doesn't matter how long it's been since we've last seen each other, we can pick up right where we left off and will be snort laughing within minutes of our reunion. Our friendship is a testament to the idea that no amount of time or distance can weaken a bond that is forged in love.

And then there are the friends you are fortunate to meet later in life. The gals at work, the women in your running group, the moms of your children's friends. How special it is to find others who understand your limited time and share your demanding schedule. Friendship at this age is just as important as in your younger years, because, despite all the joys and milestones, motherhood can be an isolating and lonely stage. Friends made during these years are friends by choice, not by circumstance, and an essential component of your sanity. The clothes may have changed (dress pants instead of miniskirts) and the priorities may have shifted (from worrying about your math test to teaching your kids long division), but the stories are just as good and the advice is even better. These are the friends who will join you at a New Kids on the Block Reunion Concert, text you a picture of themselves in a mirror for outfit approval, convince you to shake your rump at Zumba, pick up your kids from school, and join you in a good cry over a bad day. These are the friends who will share in the triumphs and tragedies of parenthood and carry you through the heartaches and ailments of middle age. They will hold your hand when you lose a loved one and walk with you around the block when you can no longer run. And when you are old and gray, they will tell you how beautiful your hair looks in the sunlight and remark how handsome your grandson is in his new school picture taped to your refrigerator—and they will mean it.

So, you'll excuse me if I got a little teary-eyed watching my daughter play with her four best friends yesterday. These girls that she shared lipsticks with today will probably be the girls she will share secrets with tomorrow. These are the girls she will tell stories to about her first kiss, her first love, her first baby. When she stops listening to my advice, these are the girls she will turn to for strength and support.  And when I'm no longer around to hold her hand, these are the women she will lean on to comfort her through the hardships of this one-way trip around the sun.

How nice it is to have friends…take the time today to tell them you appreciate their presence in your life. Send them a text, give them a call, or tell them you love them—because a life without girlfriends is like a cookie without the chocolate chips—all the work with none of the sweetness.

# SHARING THE CROWN

When I first informed my daughter that she was going to have a baby sister, her initial reaction was more suspicion than excitement. I could see the gears in her little mind turning, "*Another princess in the castle…hmmm…what does that mean for my reign?*" When told that she would have to share a bedroom with this new interloper, her suspicion turned to annoyance. "*She's sleeping in MY room?*" she asked with a jealous glance back at her brother. And when she realized that she would have to give up one of her two closets for freshly laundered pink onesies and footie pajamas, her annoyance turned to full-scale revolt. Through tears she managed to choke out, "*But that's where my dress up clothes live!*" before descending into heaving sobs of despair. The outrage! The humanity! Fast-forward two years, and the disruption has turned into a blessing. The outraged princess morphed into an overprotective big sis.

For those of you lucky enough to have a sister or two, you know this dynamic well. Relationships between sisters tend to contain the following

141

dichotomous elements: loyalty and rivalry, protection and distance, affection and annoyance, shared secrets and borrowed clothes, compassion and competition. Only sisters can be sworn enemies in the morning but soul mates by dinner. Hell hath no fury like a sister given less than equal time with the straightener before school in the morning. Yet at the same time, there is no one scarier than a woman whose sister has been wronged by another.

Growing up with a sister is both aggravating and comforting. My little sister and I shared a room from the time of her birth (I was 3 ½) until I left for college. Throughout those many years we divided our room by alternating between a line of duct tape on the floor and a hanging curtain made from a bed sheet strung over a rope nailed to two corners of our room. My Garth Brook posters were hung on one wall, her kitten posters on another. My decorative water globes on one shelf, her porcelain dolls on another. I still blame her fascination with porcelain dolls for my inability to walk into the toy room at night for fear of an unblinking army of dolls coming to life and attacking me with their unbending knee joints and fixed expressions of evil. But despite the dividing line, I remember many nights of giggles after bedtime and whispers in the moonlight. In the event of a thunderstorm or a bad dream, it was my bed she would crawl into. It was my sister who slept on the floor if I had a friend sleepover—giving up her bed so that she could still hang with the big girls. And it was my sister (and frequently our cousin Chrissy) who would cover for me as I slipped out of our bedroom window to meet up with friends at an hour well past my curfew. To her credit, she kept this "sneak out secret" until after I left for college, much to our mother's dismay and surprise.

The vast majority of my childhood memories involve my sister. Whether it was her tagging along with my friends to help out with Homecoming float building my freshman year (breaking into an impromptu dance routine to "*Whoop There It Is*" on top of the trailer in an attempt to impress the older kids), wearing matching red and green plaid dresses made by our mother to the family Christmas party (Oh, don't worry, my mom made herself one too—twinsies!), or playing catch with our dad in the side yard (usually resulting in her getting mad about a rogue throw or a missed fly ball and, subsequently, storming back into the house to fall asleep angrily in our room), she was always there—my lifelong companion.

Our lives continue parallel paths today. We both have two girls of our own. I added a boy to the mix as well and she has another bundle of joy on the way. We both settled down in our hometown to give our babies the same idyllic childhood that we enjoyed and that only small-town living can bring. We still share clothes. (Clarification: she buys cool clothes, gets tired of them, and gives them to me after a few seasons.) We still eat our parents' food and dote on our little brother. And we both plan on causing trouble together at the nursing home. We will probably share a room there and we may or may not put down a line of duct tape again to divide up our "sides." It really depends on if she plans on bringing those creepy porcelain dolls or not.

That's the beauty of sisterhood. You get a friend for life…a truth-telling, makeup sharing, hair curling, favorite dress stealing, tattle-telling, dream encouraging friend for life. So, as I look at my two girls this morning—big sister pushing little sister around in a baby doll stroller—this is what I hope for them.

I hope they continue to build the bond that has developed between them these last fifteen months. I hope they let me dress them in matching outfits for just a little while longer. I hope they crawl into each other's beds to whisper secrets past midnight and comfort each other during the stormy times of life. I hope they encourage each other along the way to make good choices but also to take chances. I hope they will have the courage to speak up if one of them starts down a dangerous path, and the strength to pull that sister back home. I hope they become each other's biggest cheerleaders, staunchest allies, and fiercest defenders. I hope they argue over clothes but miss each other when they leave for college. I hope they create as many beautiful, shared memories as I have with my sister with the one small exception of providing an alibi for sneaking out. But because I know the power of the bond between sisters, I'm getting alarms on my windows just in case.

# EVERY GIRL NEEDS A BROTHER

I'll never forget that phone call. In the spring of my sophomore year of college, I was standing in the middle of the living room in my rented house when I heard my mom's voice on the other line say, "*Hi Honey. I'm pregnant, are you mad?*"

Not the typical discussion between an 18-year-old girl and her mother but, far from upset, I was elated. My parents, high school sweethearts who'd had two daughters early in their marriage, were about to add a third "later in life" baby to the mix. And, with any luck, it would be a boy. You see, I'd been wishing for a little brother for most of my life. My sister and I were a great team, and we had a ton of fun growing up, but I always thought it would be cool to throw a boy into the equation. Someone who would be great at lifting heavy furniture when we wanted to rearrange our room and would gladly take on the responsibility of killing spiders. Every penny I threw into a well, every star that shot across the night sky, every dandelion puff I blew into the wind, the wish was always the same: *please let me have a baby brother*. I continued to wish that far beyond any reasonable amount of time and into early adulthood. Turns out my persistence (and pennies) paid off.

I returned home that summer to a glowing mama, an excited dad, and a job as a lifeguard at Pennelwood, a local summer resort that catered to city folk looking to spend a week in the woods. One hot July day, just after I'd finished the morning swimming lessons, I was beckoned to the lodge over the walkie-talkie to take a phone call from my mom. This was before the prevalence of cell phones, so I had to talk through a device connected to the wall by a curly cord. My mom had just returned from her 20-week ultrasound, and she was too excited to wait until I got home that evening to share the news—she was having a boy. Oh, the excitement that swept through our family! Her cousins threw her a baby shower (It had been 18 years since her first one) and the color blue took over all of our preparations. We even helped pick out his name, Brendan, after our favorite hockey player on the Red Wings.

That fall I went back for my junior year of college at Grand Valley State and anxiously awaited yet another phone call from my mom. It came three days after the opening of deer hunting season. I

walked through the doors of the apartment that I
shared with my best friend Emily who excitedly
informed me that my mom had just called and they
were headed to the hospital. Too excited to pack,
Em helped me throw some necessities into a
clothesbasket (the official suitcase for college
students) and followed me out the door with
instructions to drive safely and kiss the new baby
for her. I arrived at the hospital a few hours later,
just in time to see my baby brother make his
entrance into the world. I'm not trying to brag
(much), but I was the first one he looked at. And,
from that moment on, he had my heart.

Having a little brother was everything I'd
dreamed of and so much more. My parents would
bring him to visit me at school, wearing his dark
blue GVSU hoodie that I'd bought him from the
bookstore, and I would take him around to all the
apartments in my complex and show him off to my
friends. Every trip home was a roller coaster of
emotions: a few days spent snuggling with my
sidekick followed by a tearful drive back to school
with an aching in my heart from missing him
already. I loved receiving pictures of him in the
mail (before the instant sharing allowed by
Facebook and Instagram) hanging out in the stands
at my little sister's softball games, dressed as a
Bumblebee for his first Halloween, or riding with

my dad on the lawnmower. My apartment was covered with photos of his little chubby face.

When I graduated and returned home for a brief stay before moving on to the next phase of my life, I finally had a few months of constant time with my little guy.  He would hang out upstairs with me in my room and I taught him to clap at the appropriate time during the opening theme song of Friends. Now a toddler with much older siblings, my sister and I thought it was hilarious every time he repeated a naughty word, and we may have encouraged it a time or two...sorry, mom. Little did we know that he was in the process of forming a heavy dose of wit and sarcasm himself.

One of my favorite memories of Brenny Boy (yes, we still call him that) was when I brought a boyfriend over to visit for an afternoon. We were playing on the hillside at my grandma's house and my date thought it would be funny to tackle me at the bottom. We looked up to see a two-year-old sprinting down the hill as fast as his little legs could carry him, on a beeline toward us with fire in his eyes. Leaping into the air, he wrapped his arms around my date's neck and tackled him to the ground. The message was clear: nobody messes with his sister.

And THAT is why I always wanted a brother. I have a built-in protector and a "No Questions Asked" bodyguard. For life. This is not hyperbole.

Despite being 19 years his elder, he has already taken on the role of Defender-In-Chief. Last year, while I was home alone with my three children, I heard a loud bang on my door in the dark hours of the night. A little scared but not sure if I wanted to hit the police button on my alarm system; I barricaded us in my bedroom and called my first responders instead. Within four minutes (they lived 8 miles away) the cavalry arrived driving a Chevy Silverado and burnishing a deer spotting light. They made a few wide sweeps of the yard and the barn, and I soon got a call that my brother was on my front porch. I unlocked the door and there stood my 14-year-old brother in nothing but a pair of shorts and armed with his trusty 12-gauge shotgun. He smiled and said, "*Hey Sis, it's all clear.*" That's what a brother does. When his sister is in danger, he jumps out of bed, grabs his gun, and runs out of the house so fast in his underwear that his mom has to throw him a pair of shorts to put on in the truck.

I think I made the right choice in naming my son after him. My own little boy is his biggest fan, and I can't wait to see what adventures they plan together. From taking him fishing to letting him play video games in his bedroom, my brother is the kind of uncle that every seven-year-old boy dreams of. Whenever my son gets sad that he doesn't have a brother of his own (as he did during the Ninja Turtles movie and every time he sees brothers together in the locker room before a hockey game), I remind him that he already has a big brother, he just calls him Uncle. It doesn't stop my son from throwing pennies into wells and breaking chicken bones to ask for one though. I understand his desire and admire his determination: brothers are worth every wish.

This past Saturday I had the honor of pinning on my little brother's boutonnière for his very first prom. As I glanced up at his handsome face (he's taller than me now), I couldn't help but see the tiny little boy who used to run into my arms. In that instant a flood of memories rushed back: his first time on the ice, his kindergarten graduation, the time he got a battery-motorized four wheeler for Christmas and spent the next six months doing "tricks" on it in the yard, the vision of him in a diaper and his green frog boots hiding behind a tree and "hunting" for turkeys.

Soon he will be leaving for his own adventures as college and a career are in the not-too-distant future. He will return home to play with his nieces and nephews and they will cry every time he leaves to go back to school. We will sit around the summer campfires and listen to his tales and talk about his plans. One day he will even stand at the end of an aisle while the love of his life walks toward him in a flowing gown of white. He will have kids of his own and my parents will be blessed with more grandbabies to spoil. But, to me, he will always be that little guy running down the hill. I sure am glad I didn't waste all those shooting stars on something silly; I'll take a brother over a pony any day.

# TEN LESSONS FOR MY SON

Every Wednesday I drop the girls off at my grandma's house and take my son to his hockey practice. It is the only time all week that it is just the two of us—my first-born and me. For an entire hour we get to talk about whatever we want, and he doesn't even have to share my attention with two little sisters. It is on these drives I've learned about the intricacies of Minecraft, his affection for the little girl down the road, and his plans to become a scientist when he grows up. Our conversations during this routine trip serve as my window to his soul and I am so thankful to have this time with him. Because I just noticed that he's seven years old. I don't know how it happened exactly, but when I looked in the mirror yesterday, I noticed a slender-faced boy sitting in the same spot that was once occupied by a pudgy-faced toddler. My little boy with the buzz cut who knew his letter sounds at 18 months old has been replaced by a little man with a stylish spike who knows all the lyrics to the latest Justin Beiber song. They told me not to blink. They were right.

He is at such a wonderful age. He is still full of questions but also thinks he knows a little bit more than he does. He is capable of getting his own cereal, making his own bed, retrieving his own clothes (under the supervision of the fashion police, otherwise known as his little sister), and taking his own shower. He doesn't need me to zip his coat or tie his shoes anymore. He can be trusted to make solo trips to the concession stand during sporting events in our hometown and he usually brings me back the change. I no longer force him to hold my hand in the parking lot. He even hosts his own YouTube channel offering dance tutorials with original moves to the latest hit songs. (Although how I found out about this channel is a story for another day.) Yet, despite all of these "big boy" things, he still likes to cuddle up with his mom on the couch and he isn't too embarrassed to give me a kiss in front of his buddies...yet. I'm still the most important woman in his life for at least a few more years (Please, God, give me 9 or 10 more years at least before the first big crush). So, while I hold this position of prominence and honor, I intend to make it count. Here are the ten biggest lessons I hope to teach my son before he leaves the comfort and warmth of my nest.

1.  Always be a gentleman, without exception. You have two little sisters who are counting on you to provide an example for the type of boys they should allow in their lives. Open doors, pay for dinner, and get your dates home before curfew. You never know, your future girlfriend could have a big brother with a mean right hook or an overprotective dad with a gun collection. Treat her like you would want your sisters to be treated and love her like you would want your future daughter to be loved.

2.  A firm handshake and eye contact are the most important components of a good first impression. Confidence comes from the eyes. Don't waste your time on a witty line or a rehearsed introduction. When it comes to first impressions, people will judge you before you ever open your mouth.

3.  Don't take the easy way out. Anything worth anything requires hard work, dedication, and sometimes a little sacrifice. This is true about careers, relationships, and parenting. Don't get me wrong, every day shouldn't be drudgery, but don't expect constant rainbows either. The tough ones stick to it and stay with the long game, knowing the finished product will be worth the effort.

4.  But don't be afraid to change your mind. If you don't like the direction, you're headed in, take a

different road. If you don't like your job, find a new one. If you aren't happy chasing this dream, find another one to run after. Life is about choices, and we are blessed to live in a nation that allows us the freedom to choose our own path. You only get one trip around the sun so don't be afraid to change seats if you don't like the scenery. Life is too precious a commodity to waste it on stale dreams and bumpy roads.

5. Don't be a slob. Pick up your clothes and do your own laundry. Dishes go in the dishwasher, not on the counter. Your future wife will want a partner, not another child to take care of. And even if you never marry, I'm not coming to your house to clean it for you—real men know how to use a broom.

6. What you do during the day you will have to sleep with at night. A man with a clear conscience gets a full night's rest. If you want to know what integrity is, just look at your papa. Take note when he gives his word to somebody and pay attention when he makes good on his promise. At the end of the day, you are only as good as your word—so make sure it means something.

7. Be involved. Take an active role in your life and contribute to your community. You'd be amazed at what can get done if you just get to doing it. Be present in your relationships and be attentive in your conversations. Be the kind of husband that

takes long walks with his wife and the kind of father that coaches his kid's sports team.

8. Don't be a jerk. You're good at things, but don't trump up your own importance—there is nothing less attractive than an arrogant man. Understand the difference between pride and pomposity. Always be kind to those who make a living serving others and, for goodness sake, never tip less than 20%.

9. Learn how to fix things that break around a house. Own a hammer and a drill, a ladder and a shovel. It sounds old fashioned, I know, but a man should have a toolbox in the garage and know how to read a measuring tape. And an axe, you should definitely own one of those. How else are you going to cut wood for papa's fire when he's too old to do it himself?

10. Be you. I don't care what your "thing" is; I just want you to know that you have the freedom to pursue it. Know that I will love you deeply regardless of the sports you play, the music you like, the friends you choose, and the clothes you wear. That sounds silly and obvious to say, but there will come a time when you will have to make a choice that might not be what your father or I would have chosen for you. Do it anyway. The only person you can be is yourself and I promise to never ask you to be anybody else.

So, sweet boy, the sky is the limit, and you are just learning how to open your wings. Soon, much too soon for this mama's liking, you will take flight and test them out a bit. And when you do, I will be there cheering you on, with a reserved seat in the front row and a net to catch you if you fall.

But, thankfully, today is not that day. No, today you held my hand while I walked you up the stairs to tuck you into bed. Today you said that you couldn't wait to take me to Mother-Son Movie Night sponsored by your elementary school next week. Today you still believe that you are going to build a house right next to mine when you get older. Today you told me, "*Mom, if I wasn't your kid, I would run away from my home until I found you.*" Today you are still my baby and I still have a few road trips until I have to share you with the world.

# THE UNCLES ARE COMING TO TOWN

Every December, my kids desperately await the return of two men from the north. One of the travelers drives a sleigh pulled by the horsepower of 300 mustangs. The other flies through the sky on a 747 bound from Minneapolis to Chicago. They come bearing gifts and good cheer and their entrance guarantees endless hours of fun. My kids count down the days until their visit and no Christmas is complete until they pull into grandma's driveway. And while they may not don red suits or wear funny fur hats, their arrival is anticipated more than the big man himself. Forget Santa, the uncles are coming to town.

I can't say I blame them. My dad's two brothers—Dave and John—have been the lives of the party for as long as I can remember. They've invented more games than Milton Bradley and their creativity could even make Walt Disney feel inadequate. One of my earliest memories involves a game that can only be described as dodge ball with stuffed animals. Uncle Dave and Uncle John (joined by Dan, the youngest brother of the family) would instruct my sister and I to gather all our plush toys and collect them in a pile on the floor. As they launched the stuffed treasures as ammunition, my sister and I would race between the open doorway, trying to dodge and weave between alternating Carebears and My Little Ponies hurled by the trifecta of uncles. A hit to the leg would require us to hop on the remaining one for round two. If both legs were hit, we would be forced to crawl between the safety zones. And the ultimate hit, and a direct shot to the head, would start the game over. Not your average game of tag, but a Dodson Family Classic that has transferred down to successive generations.

Have you ever sled on a homemade luge? Probably not, because the construction of such a massive project would require hours of shoveling and packing. But if you had my uncles, you would assume that a luge was just a normal part of Christmas Break. They spend days (not an exaggeration) shoveling snow and designing a slick surface 40 yards long, complete with sides and tunnels and a deadman's curve. With Christmas lights strung along the top for decoration, nieces and nephews take their turns down the slope as night falls, traveling at speeds faster than they should and winding up in snowbanks (if they follow the path) or the woods (if they miss their exit). Despite cousin Rachel's launch into a patch of briars one year and Uncle Dave's face plant into a wall of ice the next, the luge remains a big hit. Needless to say, this unseasonably warm weather has really put a damper on our normal holiday routine. On the bright side, this might be the first Christmas in memory without any facial lacerations or concussions.

As you can probably tell, the uncles bring the magic and leave happy kids in their wake. Their latest game that the cousins clamor for as soon as they walk through the door is called "Ogre Angry." It goes like this: the uncles arm themselves with pillows and wear blindfolds and the kids take their places behind couches and dressers. The uncles then turn into angry ogres (complete with growls) and blindly swing the pillows around in attempts to connect with the poor peasants of the village. You should know that this description is much tamer than the original version. Ogre Angry first debuted with the older nieces and nephews and looked more like a game of kick the can on steroids with the Ogres (still blindfolded) protecting a lit candle hidden inside a coffee tin. The game was played outside and at night, with many obstacles positioned shin height and many collisions with melted wax.

Lest you think that the uncles only save their fun for the kids, let me inform you that these two masterminds have designed and created my ugly Christmas sweater for the last four years. I'm not talking about cute little sweaters with embroidered snowmen and attached jingling bells. No, these creations are works of art and get bolder and wilder every year. The first year involved a Goodwill sweater with glass ornaments attached courtesy of Uncle Dave's expert suturing skills mastered in medical school. They stepped up their game year two and attached a wooden train track in a circle along the bottom of the sweater and included a battery-powered train to ride along the track. That was SUPER fun to pick up off the floor every time I made a sudden move. Year three was epic, and they started the project a month in advance. Uncle Dave drew, painted, and meticulously cut out at least a thousand tiny reindeer and attached them with hot glue to a snow-covered field of pine trees across the shoulders of my sweater. After receiving this sweater, I was convinced that there would be nothing that could top this creation. But I should have known better. The night before the last day of school before Christmas Break, I received two very large packages. One included two hand carved wooden swords painted and adorned in the spirit of Christmas. The other included the armor. Red lacquered shin and arm guards, body armor and a helmet all constructed from paper mache. For an entire day I was the Christmas Warrior…and it was glorious.

So, this Christmas, as our family gathers around the fire to tell stories and play games, I can assure you that our party will include a rousing game of mafia, a few rounds of winker, and an angry ogre or two. Uncle John (lawyer by day, superhero by night) will provide countless pulls on the sleigh. He doesn't even need a wintry mix on the ground to drag the sled…he found out years ago that if he sprays cooking oil on the bottom, it will go faster than any snow packed hill. And Uncle Dave, normally a physician in Minnesota, will substitute Pictionary for patients and art projects for doctor's visits. And the jolly old man from the North Pole will come and go and the kids will probably notice him…as long as he doesn't interfere with their current module of Dungeons and Dragons.

# THAT'S WHAT DADS DO

When we moved into our new home, my husband's first project was to construct a two-story swing by suspending cables between two tall trees in our backyard. For three consecutive nights, he'd head out to the backyard, armed with a flood light, a ladder, and a mission. On the final night, he emerged victorious in the girls' room just after they'd drifted off to sleep to make his big announcement…the swing was ready.

My oldest son was still awake, so he became the de-facto test pilot for his stepdad and, along with our infant son, the four of us raced outside at 9:30 pm to give it a whirl. As our feet touched the night sky and the wind rustled through our pajamas, I reflected on how dads always seem to bring out the fun in life. Bedtime could wait.

I've been surrounded by great examples of fatherhood at every stage of my life. I was blessed with a grandpa who regularly took me fishing and blackberry picking and never missed a single ball game. He spent hours talking with me about world events and my plans for the future, using his reporter skills to question and analyze every angle of every decision. It is from him that I learned the importance of critical thought and the value of an open mind. I never beat him at finishing the crossword puzzles from the newspaper, and I only came close to beating him in a rice around the ice rink once. He gave me my first copy of <u>The Hobbit</u> and shared my love for Harry Potter. Many of my sweetest childhood memories were spent walking in the woods by his side. I only wish he were still here to share these lessons and moments with my own children—they would've adored him as much as I did.

My grandpa's involvement and devotion were traits passed down to my own father. My dad was the guy who organized the neighborhood wiffle ball game and coached the little league softball team. He was the rules enforcer, the curfew police, and the supplier of allowance money, giving my sister and I each a ledger from The Bank of Dad from which we could make deposits and withdrawals to learn the concept of balancing an account. My dad is a natural educator, always looking for the "teachable moment" in everyday life. In fifth grade, he took me to school early one morning to retrieve and complete the homework I'd forgotten there the night before. In the parking lot, he made me sign a contract stating that I would take full responsibility of any future missing assignments should I ever neglect to bring my work home again. This early morning trip would be a one-time event.

Lest you think he played the role of constant taskmaster, let me reassure you that he also relished the role of Embarraser-in-Chief. In seventh grade, when a pre-teen girl would rather die than have her parents drop her off in front of the middle school, my dad would let me off at the corner and then follow slowly beside me in his truck, honking and waving and yelling out the window, "Daddy loves you!" What was the lesson here? Some possible options include: 1. To learn not to take myself so seriously, 2. To urge me to laugh in the face of peer pressure and judgmental adolescents, or 3. To know that, even if I didn't always want him there, he would always be there—by my side, and cheering me on.

Whenever I am faced with what seems to be an insurmountable obstacle, he is the voice inside my head urging me to keep pushing, keep climbing, keep going. I still call him when weighing the options of an impending decision, and he's the leader of a half-dozen minions who call him Papa and follow him around in the woods. And, despite his questionable fashion choices and collection of garage-sale shirts, he is the coolest guy in town.

As any mother will tell you, it's impossible to overstate the importance of a father in the life of his children. His daughters will measure every boy by the standard he sets; his sons will emulate his actions and follow his lead. He is the one that carries little bodies upstairs when they've fallen asleep on the couch, the one who will teach them about football and how to drive a car, and the one they will call years from now when they run out of gas on the highway. He will be their provider and protector long after they leave the nest.

That's what dads do. They fuel your fire and encourage your passions. They lift you up into trees and stand on the ground, far enough away to give you a taste of independence but close enough to catch you if you fall. They hold onto the back of your bike and let go at just the right time. They sneak lessons into everyday life and hold up the moon. And even if they do it all in camouflage crocs, they usually stop for ice cream on the way home and let you swing past bedtime.

# WHY I STILL NEED MY MOM

I call my mom at least twice a week to ask the most random questions that I'm convinced only she can answer. Questions like, "*How can I tell if this hamburger meat is still good*" or "*Is it really necessary to hand wash this shirt or is that just a suggestion?*" or "*So, what does poison ivy look like again?*"

Remember when you were younger, and you misplaced something and your mom always seemed to know where it was? Chances are she still possesses that power. It's an even greater chance that her unique role as the only person in the house capable of locating missing items has since been passed down to you. It is only now, as a mother myself, that I can truly appreciate the level of annoyance that comes with being designated as the "All-Time Finder of All Things." A few days ago, I spent a full hour searching for Uni the Unicorn's magical berry. This is an hour of my life that I will never get back.

Like most mother-daughter relationships, our partnership has progressed through all of the traditional stages. As a child I was her bike-riding sidekick and Christmas tree decorating assistant. As a bratty pre-teen, she made sure my softball uniform was always clean and I made sure to invite a herd of my cereal-eating friends over without warning to drive up her grocery bill. As a know-it-all teenager, I lamented her rules while benefiting from her unwavering support and constant care. It wasn't until my college years that I finally realized how much I missed her homemade mashed potatoes and around the clock laundry service. In my 20s she was my biggest cheerleader, my staunchest defender, and my shopping partner. And now, as a mother in my mid-30s, I rely on her guidance and assistance more than ever.

I can't tell you how many urgent calls I've made during the last seven years that have resulted in her jumping in her car and driving over to help. When my son split his chin open on the shower rail, I called her on speakerphone while I held him wrapped in a towel on my lap and waited for her arrival and opinion to determine if he needed to go to the hospital for stitches. She volunteered to take my daughter who was, by this time, sitting in a cold bath and wondering why her crazy mother was crying. A year before this, she drove to my house in record time when I called to report that my daughter had cut her nose on a can of corn while playing in the pantry when I was cooking dinner. (I swear I am not a negligent mother; my kids are just a tad bit clumsy.) Not to leave my youngest out, my mom was the first person I called when the doctor came in on my baby's first day in this world to inform me that she might be transferred to the ICU. Without having to ask, my mom (who had stayed the night before until 3 a.m. to witness her birth) raced back to the hospital and spent the day rocking the baby and reassuring me that everything would be fine. And it was—mamas always know. It's nice to have a nana on call to swoop in with reassuring words and a calming presence that makes everyone, myself included, feel better. She also buys Band-Aids in bulk to fix a variety of scrapes (real and imagined) and delivers popsicles and 7-Up to sick grandbabies who are more than just a little bit spoiled.

It's not until I became a mother that I realized just how labor-intensive that job really is. I always wondered why my mom was ready for bed by 9:00. I thought she was just a party pooper, but it turns out she was understandably exhausted from a full day spent working and cleaning, cooking and carpooling. Her day began hours before the rest of us woke up and she's kept this same schedule for the last 34 years as my youngest brother is a freshman in high school and a few years away from leaving the nest. And now I know that Moms really don't have "sick days" because, after all, the laundry won't fold itself and for some reason the kids think they need to eat every day.

The influence of a mother is impossible to understate. Her example becomes your habit, and her voice becomes your own. Have you ever opened your mouth to speak and out pops one of your mother's characteristic phrases? I frequently tell my children that I want to "squeeze their guts out." The first time I said it, my kids looked at me in horror and disbelief until I explained that this means I love them so much that I want to give them a big squeezer hug. (Some phrases tend to get lost in translation, but you get my point.) A mother is a beacon in the night and the calm in the storm. She can simultaneously serve as both a confidant and a critic, your biggest supporter and your most cautious advisor. She can mend broken hearts with trips to the mall and cure boredom with marathons of reality TV and homemade popcorn doused with unspeakable amounts of butter. A mother sews ripped prom dresses and pays for wedding gowns. She makes your favorite cake for your birthday (fresh coconut crème) and buys diet pop when you are coming over for dinner. She knows your greatest secrets and has borne witness to your darkest hours, and still loves you all the same. Over the years, a mother dries your tears and a few of her own. And she holds the unique position of having changed both your diapers and those of your children.

So, as I pause to reflect on my blessings and give thanks for the wonderful people in my life, I want to send out a special thank you to all of the moms who sacrifice their own needs for those of their children.

Thank you for staying up late to help with homework and getting up early to make breakfast. Thank you for spending your days in the boardroom and your nights in the bleachers. Thank you for skipping showers and hair appointments to make it to gymnastics. A special thanks to all of you single mothers who must also play the part of dad and bear the full weight and responsibility of parenthood—I am in awe of your selflessness and amazed by your strength. To the moms who marry into motherhood and assume the role with grace and dignity, thank you for showing the world that love isn't bound by bloodline. And for those of you that welcome children into your arms that you didn't carry in your wombs, you are proof that a mother's love is unconditional and the world could use a few more women like you. And for the moms who are watching from Heaven, we search for your guidance in our hearts and your absence is felt daily. Even though we wish we could hear your voice just one more time, we know that you are making our favorite cake in preparation for our glorious reunion and rocking our babies before you send them down to us.

And, to my own mom, thank you for setting the standard for what a mother should be and for loving my babies as your own. I even forgive you for loading them up with cookies and sweet tea before sending them back home. I recognize karmic justice when I see it.

# TIME MARCHES ON

I still remember the song that was playing as I drove my little red Hyundai Excel down the highway, packed floorboard to ceiling with clothes and shoes, bound for Kalamazoo and my new life as a college student. I sang "Wide Open Spaces" at the top of my lungs along with the Dixie Chicks and must have played that track on the CD six more times before I reached my final destination. The words of the chorus rang out so true – "*She needs wide open spaces, room to make big mistakes, new faces, she knows the high stakes.*" The world was my oyster, full of promise and possibilities. I could choose my own destiny. When I look back at that memory through the eyes of a seventeen-year-old, I can still feel the excitement of that drive. When I look back at that memory through the eyes of a mother, however, I get a different feeling. It's funny how perspective changes everything.

Instead of seeing the college bound Co-Ed rushing around her room, throwing all of her favorite sweaters and framed pictures into her suitcase, I see a mother on the other side of the door, holding back tears as she stares at a picture on the wall of her now grown daughter as a five-year-old, splashing in the waves during a day spent at the beach. Instead of the Dixie Chicks, I hear Whitney Houston's "*Greatest Love of All*" playing from the tape deck of an old minivan as a Mom recalls the countless hours spent listening to her daughters singing in the backseat on the way to school or sports practices or sleepovers. Instead of feeling excitement for the future, I feel the distinct sensation of sadness and loss with a heavy dose of teary-eyed nostalgia. Sure, the sadness is mixed with pride, at the person this young girl is and will become, but the sadness is still there, nonetheless.

They don't call it an empty nest for nothing; our children hold our hearts and when they leave us, either to head off to kindergarten or to college, we feel an emptiness in our homes as well as our chests.

A few years ago my friend Becky, whose kids are older than mine, told me that she felt like the years sped up as soon as her children entered school. She said, "It's like the time goes to warp speed as soon as kindergarten hits and, the next thing you know, your oldest is entering high school." To be honest, I was in the haze of having two young children, so I didn't really believe her when she said that time was going to progress at anything faster than a snail's pace. If you've spent any time at home with two babies under two, you know how one hour can feel like five. But now I know. Now I believe her. Because I swear, I was just teaching my little man his letters but, somehow, he will walk through the first grade classroom doors as a reader of chapter books. And that sweet, dimpled baby that I rocked to sleep every night (wasn't that just yesterday?) will be starting kindergarten in nine days.

It's funny how the realization that our children are growing up can strike at the most unexpected times. The other night I let the kids fall asleep in my bed, just so I could snuggle them a little bit longer. As I picked up my daughter to carry her to her own bed, I was shocked by how long her legs were and how they dangled from my arms as I navigated the stairs and doorways. When did she get so big? How did I not notice this before? I actually cried as I looked at her face and realized that those chubby baby cheeks had been replaced by the thinned-out version of a young girl. I didn't cry because she was getting bigger and growing at a normal and healthy pace, those are good things and should be celebrated. I cried because I didn't notice it every day. I cried because it snuck up on me. I cried because I could only vaguely remember the way her little mouth stayed partially open when she slept as a baby. I cried because as much as I wanted her legs to grow, I equally wanted to go back to a time where I could cradle her entire body in my arms. The dichotomous nature of a parent is almost too much to bear sometimes.

I know that we shouldn't say these things out loud. That we want our children to stay little forever. That we want them to stay safe within the four walls of our home. That we don't want them to venture out into the real world; a place that can be cruel and cold and unforgiving. We think these things, every parent does. As we lie awake in the stillness of the night, we think about all the ways we can build a wall to protect our babies from the pain and heartbreak they will inevitably face throughout their lives. Sure, we think these thoughts. But do you know why we shouldn't say them out loud? Because we know that, in our heart of hearts, they are statements made from fear and selfishness and not grounded in reality. They will grow up. They will leave our homes to build their own. They will get their hearts broken. They will experience loss. But it will be beautiful. It will be life. And, God willing, we will get to watch it all and be right there to cheer them on.

My dear friend Renee is sending her youngest child off to her freshman year of college today. You would be hard-pressed to find a warmer, kinder, more nurturing mother than my friend, so you can imagine the turmoil her heart has undergone during the lead up to this big day. She's done all she could to prepare her daughter for this next step and, by all measures, she's succeeded. She and her husband have raised a poised, confident, and incredibly talented young woman who will surely exceed all expectations. Yet, my heart aches for Renee because I can only imagine the dueling feelings of pain and pride that will tug at her heart as she watches her baby girl climb the stairs to her dorm room. It is hard to let go of something you love more than yourself. But it is even harder to try to hang on to the winds of change. Best just to hug them tight, tell them you love them, and hold back the tears until you get back to the car.

I'm beginning to realize that it doesn't matter which phase our children are entering, all new steps in life will result in a crying mother behind the steering wheel of her parked car or a misty eyed father whose voice will crack just a little bit as he's giving last minute advice. I was that mother last year as I watched my oldest walk confidently into his kindergarten classroom on his first day and I'll be that mother again when my daughter does the same next week. I will be that mother when my baby, the last to leave my nest, throws her high school graduation cap high into the air. I will definitely be that mother who cries in the front row while she watches her daughters walk down the aisle. And I will proudly be that grandma who takes her son's newborn baby into her arms for the first time.

Time marches on. We can either drag our feet, kicking and screaming, hoping that our persistence will slow its passage, or we can march right along with it—enjoying the view and the changing scenery along the way. Just remember to tuck a few tissues into your hiking shorts.

# NINJAS IN THE PASTA AISLE

What happens to children when they enter a grocery store?  You can have all the pre-game talks in the car that you want about appropriate store behavior.  You can threaten them with trumped up consequences that will be doled out if they decide not to follow your guidelines.  If you're desperate enough (and I usually am), you can even agree to a special treat to come at the end in exchange for good behavior.

We perform these pre-store rituals with hope in our hearts and dread in our bones. We know that our pleas will fall on deaf ears.  Our sweet cherubs will look at us all doe-eyed and nod their heads through the lecture and maybe even throw in a couple "yes mamas," but right before we enter through the automatic doors, they will uncover the vials hidden in their vest pockets, drink the gummy bear juice, and away they will go – bouncing here and there and everywhere.

I know it's going to happen. I know it every single time and yet I still subject myself to the torture that is grocery shopping with three kids. I perpetually live in the denial stage and have yet to move on to acceptance when it comes to this part of parenting. What is that old saying about the definition of insanity?

Let's just look at the latest example as a case study so that we can further examine my level of mental instability. With two diapers left in the house, I decided to venture out last night to grab "just the necessities." It would be a quick trip I told myself (oh, the valley of denial is deep), in and out. My barnacle baby was extra clingy last night so I decided to grab a small cart since her little tentacles weren't unwrapping from my neck anytime soon to sit in the seat. Upon entering the store, my daughter exclaimed, "*I'll push the cart*" and, against my better judgment, I relented. (Some days I'm just too tired to fight the good fight.) Thirty seconds later, she had managed to run into the metal structure holding the giant bouncing balls, the Krispy Kreme donut shelf, and her brother's left heel.

Assuming control of the cart (pushing with one hand, holding the baby with the other), we made our way down the first aisle – this time in a straight line. My daughter spotted a seemingly glow in the dark liquid and made a beeline for it. She then screamed back at me and anyone else within 200 yards, "*Mom, can we get this blue drink!?! I LOVE this blue drink and nana always has it at her house!*" And so begins my weekly run through the seven circles made famous by Dante. A 20-minute Survival Style obstacle course of bobbing and weaving through aisles, attempting to avoid the "hot spots" that will lead to the downfall of this trip (read: cereal aisle and chip aisle), and repeating the same phrase over and over in robotic fashion – "*No, put it back, we are not getting that. I don't care if nana let you get it last time.*"

Sometimes, when I have the energy, I try to make it into a game. I pretend it's a scavenger hunt and give them items to pluck off the shelf and put into the cart as we make our way down each row. Sometimes this works. Usually, it devolves into a pouting fest for my four-year-old who is mad that her ultra-competitive brother got to the box of fruit snacks before she could. But I digress.

Halfway through last night's escapade, my son's tolerance for shopping reached its breaking point and his normally sweet, rule-following nature was replaced by a crazed ninja, compelled to practice the ancient moves of Master Splinter in the pasta lined Dojo. Using the side of the cart as a springboard, he launched himself into the air, flying dragon style. He grabbed the box of spaghetti, now doubling as a katana blade, and deftly sliced and diced the air around him. After I examined the pasta sauce choices for way too long (and ended up selecting the same one as always), I barked at him to re-sheath his sword. And he did, but slowly….and only after making one last valiant lunge at his pouty sister.

Now let's pause here to discuss the cart situation. At some point throughout the trip, I will have multiple monkeys hanging off the sides. This is a tricky situation because, A. at least I can control their movements if they are attached to my cart, but B. they think it's really fun to lean back while still holding on, thus taking out a row of Pringles containers. At least we aren't at the store with the car carts because, great idea and all, but those are the worst.

Back to the trip. Somehow, I'd managed to deposit every item on my list (and plenty of items not on my list) into my cart and, as I rounded the end cap to the last aisle, I began to breathe a little easier. The finish line was near – there was light at the end of the tunnel – I could see the checkout register. But what a rookie mistake this thought was. Just as I grabbed the extra-large container of coffee creamer, I saw a flash of a ninja run into the beer cooler. This is a separate refrigerated room, placed strategically at the end of the last aisle as if to say to parents – *"Don't forget to grab a six pack on your way out. I've seen your kids in the store, go ahead, you deserve it."* Alas, this store is not set up like a Costco's and there is no sampling station with a kind little old woman saying, "*Would you like to try a sample of Oberon*?" I ventured in to fetch my six-year-old warrior from the frozen tundra, other two in tow and, as I emerged from the cooler, I slammed right into someone I knew. Luckily on this trip I only swung the door into the cart of my sweet Aunt Barb who understood why I was doing the walk of shame out of the beer cooler with three kids under the age of six. Usually, though, it's a school board member, a former or (even worse) current student, or some other pillar of the community.

Having achieved the height of my embarrassment and top blood pressure level, we finally made our way to the check-out counter. My kids love unloading the cart unto the conveyer belt and I happily obliged because my left arm was already about to fall off from holding a 20-pound thumb-sucker for the last 20 minutes. Never mind that the can of soup always ends up slammed on top of the bread. No problem that they prefer to stack the yogurts to ensure that one or two will topple onto the floor. They are helping, and what mom can resist a modicum of assistance. As the contents of the cart were emptied and the sub-total was displayed on the screen (how did I spend that much? I was just coming to get milk and eggs! Where did those cookies come from?) I thought to myself, "Y*ou did it. You survived. You deserve a* *medal or a plaque with your name on it, or at least an uninterrupted glass of wine.*" I ignored the sound of my children hitting every button on the instant lotto machine, paid the nice lady, and pushed my overflowing cart of plastic bags toward freedom.

As the fresh air of the outside world hit my face, I noticed a mother just entering with her brood. I recognized the anxiety on her face and, as we exchanged sympathetic glances, we both realized that this too shall pass.

As much as we dread these weekly trips, someday much too soon, we will resume solo trips to the store. Our carts will hold less – a pound of hamburger instead of three, a box of Raisin Bran instead of Lucky Charms. We will gaze at the harried mother in the canned goods aisle with a pang of misty-eyed nostalgia. We will remember fondly the time when our little ones hung off the carts and knocked down the bags of goldfish. When we get to that point, will you make a pact with me to offer to hold her baby while she attempts to reach the green beans off the top shelf? And as we hand her squirmy baby back to her, promise you'll join me in whispering, "*You're doing good Mama.*" Because sometimes all it takes is a kind word from a battle-hardened veteran to help us realize that we are all in this together. And don't judge her if you spot a bottle of chardonnay hidden under the diapers, desperate times call for desperate measures.

# THE CHEERIOS HAVE GONE ROGUE

I must pick up a hundred rogue Cheerios a day. Forget ants or ladybugs, I have a Cheerio infestation. They are everywhere – from the couch cushions to the bathroom floor (sometimes you gotta have snacks when you're waiting for your turn in the shower) to the car seats. But this one, this colorful one that had adhered itself so completely to the kitchen floor underneath the baby's highchair, was giving me a run for my money. No matter how hard I tried to wedge it from its permanent home on my hardwoods, I could not get it to break loose. I finally had to find a flat head screwdriver and employ angles and force to pry this sugary circle apart from its impressive hold. See kids, you totally use Geometry after high school.

It was probably a good thing that I spent so much time on my kitchen floor this morning because, while I was down there, I noticed a puddle of dried up apple sauce that looked to be a bit older than just last night's dinner. After I wiped that up with the baby's cloth diaper rag dipped into my son's water cup (out of paper towels...again), I caught a glimpse of a half-eaten broccoli stalk and a few errant drops of cranberry juice hanging out together under my daughter's chair. Let me tell you, the surprises didn't end there. I had opened a Pandora's Box of scraps from the past. So, I did what any responsible mother would do. I got up off the floor and went into the living room. Out of sight, out of mind.

I had this grand vision I would spend my yearlong maternity leave of absence in a well-kept home with sparkling floors and nutritious home cooked meals every night. The laundry would be folded and put away as soon as the buzzer rang on the dryer. The bathrooms would smell of rosebuds and disinfectant. My pantry would be organized and my closets would be color coordinated. Company coming? No need to call ahead – my house would always be spotless and ready for entertaining. Why wouldn't it be? After all, I was going to be home ALL DAY with nothing else to do. I'd managed to keep my house semi-clean with two kids and a full-time job; surely, I could do better with just one extra kid and staying at home. My plan just had one tiny little flaw. I was going to be home ALL DAY. This meant that my kids were going to be making messes ALL DAY and I was going to be following them around cleaning up after them ALL DAY. Oh, and one extra kid meant adding a billion times more laundry. Cute little pink onesies and adorable little lacy socks, but still....

So, what is a modern mother to do? How can I devote time to my family and career without allowing my house to look like an episode of Hoarders? Like everything else, I guess it's all about moderation. Do I dust regularly? Nope. Unless, of course, you consider twice a year to be regular. If so, then you and I can be best friends. Do I always use the attachments on my vacuum cleaner to sweep the corners or the baseboards? Not a chance. Do I change the filter on the water dispenser in my refrigerator every time the red light comes on? Just did...so I'm probably good for another three years. But my kids have clean shirts to wear, they eat vegetables with dinner most nights of the week (a corndog is technically a vegetable since it has one in its name, right?) and they have fresh sheets to sleep on. They are happy and healthy and capable of making huge messes all on their very own. So, what if the inside of my microwave looks like the one from the set of the Gremlins, just don't warm anything up when you come over to visit next time.

As I stare at the mountain of clothes piling up on my chaise lounge, waiting to be reunited with hangers and drawers, I remind myself that there won't always be that many towels and t-shirts to put away. I might sigh at the list of chores to be finished tonight before I retire to my pillow, lunches to be packed and coffee to be made, but at least I have people who depend on those chores. And if the clothes are still there tomorrow because I chose to take an impromptu trip to the beach or play hockey using the laundry basket for a goal, well, then that will be okay too. There will always be more socks to sort and more sinks to rinse.

Whenever I feel overwhelmed by the enormity of the task of keeping a clean house, I walk into my bedroom and read the sign hanging on the wall by my rocking chair. On it is written an old saying, probably from a woman who had cobwebs in her corners but kids on her lap. I'll share it with you – it's easy enough to remember.

*Cleaning and scrubbing can wait 'til tomorrow,*
*For babies grow up, we've learned to our sorrow,*
*So quiet down cobwebs, dust go to sleep*
*I'm rocking my baby, and babies don't keep.*

# BREAKING UP WITH MONDAY

It's been one of those days. The kind of day that you can appreciate with all five of your senses.

We were already on the road to hockey camp this morning (running late, per usual) when I noticed that my gas gauge was in the danger zone. Seven miles to go before an empty tank and 12 miles remaining to get to the ice rink. I'm no math major, but even I knew enough to take the nearest exit and fill 'er up. I parked the van and stepped out into the beginnings of a major thunderstorm.

Ever the multi-tasker, I decided to take the next minute of free time – while the gas pump was simultaneously filling up my tank and draining my bank account – to do a pre-bus of the kid zone of my van. I noticed a to-go cup sitting in the back row cup holder. Hmm, I thought, that's odd. We were at Dunkin Donuts four days ago, what could possibly be in that cup? And then, like a lightning bolt from the darkening sky, it hit me. Chocolate milk. The days old cup was holding curdled, disgusting, smelly chocolate milk. Willing myself not to look at the contents of the transparent plastic container, I grabbed it with the intent of getting it out of my vehicle as fast as possible. This tactic was, in hindsight, a big mistake. In my haste, I slammed my elbow against the back of the passenger seat and dropped the cup on the carpet. In my version of the events, this all happened in slow motion, and I let out a long, "*Noooooo!!!*" before the brown, curdled liquid exploded onto my gray interior. The smell was immediate. Both kids responded with overdramatized shrieks of horror, and I just stood there. Disbelief was soon replaced by rage, and it took me a full 30 seconds to realize that I needed to get it out of the carpet. So, like any mother, I grabbed the one item that can be trusted to clean up any mess – a baby wipe. Nine wipes and a few choice words later, and we were back on the road to our original destination, with the windows rolled all the way down.

This is what Monday smells like.

If today were a movie, the first scene with the chocolate milk would be what my high school English teacher referred to as foreshadowing. Nostrils sufficiently damaged, we finally arrived at the ice rink with a few minutes to spare. I laced up my son's skates, slapped the helmet on his head, threw him his stick and waved goodbye. Baby in stroller and big sister in hand, we stepped out into the lobby only to be welcomed by the roaring sound of a downpour on the metal roof. I had one of those, *"well, shoot"* moments where I debated between: A. staying in the lobby with the girls until the rain let up a bit, or B. braving the torrential rains for the time that it would take us to cross the parking lot. Maybe I was feeling adventurous or, more likely, I was thinking about all the chores that were waiting for me at home, but we chose the latter. I put the baby's blanket over her head (she immediately pulled it off), grabbed sister's hand a little tighter, opened the doors and ran. If Noah's Ark had been parked next to my van in the parking lot, I wouldn't have been the least bit surprised.

Two steps before we reached the van, the biggest clap of thunder I have ever heard in my life caused all three of us to scream. That is not an exaggeration. The baby screamed, sister screamed, and I (the one who is in charge of protecting them) screamed like a girl in a horror movie. In my defense, it was really dang loud. By the time I got both girls safely buckled in, I was drenched, and they were hysterical. Sister was screaming and the baby was genuinely frightened. I climbed up into the front seat and pressed the ignition button. And then I remembered the stroller that was now doubling as a five-gallon bucket outside. I readied myself to dodge the lightning bolts, opened the door, and threw the stroller (still fully assembled) into the back. When I returned to my seat, I reflected on the irony of the situation. As a mother of three, there are many days that go by where I don't get the chance to take a shower. It was only 9:00 a.m. and I had just had my second one of the day.

This is what Monday feels like.

Safely home, I began to prepare our lunch. Mealtime is not generally a fun time at our house. As someone who will eat basically anything, I've managed to raise the pickiest eaters this side of the Mason-Dixon. But, today, I was ready. The menu was packed with my go-to, pre-approved items that were sure to please everyone. I made a hot dog for sister (no bun please, just a giant puddle of ketchup), warmed up peas for the baby, and cut up watermelon for both. I asked my dear daughter to set the table and she even retrieved waters for all of us. Things were turning around it seemed. It was going to be a lovely lunch! With both girls happily munching, I sat down to enjoy my hotdog and took a monstrous bite. As I was chewing, I looked down at my plate and noticed that the color of the bun was a bit off. The normal light brown color had been replaced by a hue of blue with a fuzzy texture. Yep, the entire bottom of the bun was covered in mold. On the bright side, I think I'm all set on penicillin for the next year.

This is what Monday tastes like.

The rest of the day passed without incident. That is, until my oldest two children were reunited after hockey camp. They were in the presence of each other for all of five minutes before the arguing began. Round one was a debate over whether the tennis racket in the garage had an 'M' or a 'W' on it. You would think this issue would be simple to resolve, given that it is a Wilson racket. Alas, my daughter can't stand to be wrong and argued her position for a full 15 minutes. Even after I broke the bad news that it was, in fact, a 'W' on the racket, she dismissed my verdict with a curt, "*I still think it's an M.*" Round two included a heated discussion regarding crayon colors. Was the crayon in question peach or was it orange? It was the Cold War all over again as the Iron Curtain descended upon my house this afternoon. The two sides were dug in deep, and the threat of mutually assured destruction was not acting as a deterrent today. After round three, a disagreement over which song from the Teen Beach 2 soundtrack should be played first for their living room dance party, I stepped in and exiled them to their separate rooms – with the demilitarized zone of their shared hallway in between them.

This is what Monday sounds like.

After dinner, I figured I was in the home stretch. T minus two hours before bedtime. What could possibly go wrong? So naïve. So utterly naïve. I asked the two older kids to keep an eye on their baby sister so I could put away the leftovers and rinse off the dishes. How is it that two minutes can be all that is needed to mess up a house that has taken me two hours to clean? I loaded the last plate and returned to the living room to find all the magazines pulled out of the basket, all the previously folded clothes scattered across the floor, and the contents of a new bottle of baby lotion soaking into the carpet. She didn't get the nickname "Babyzilla" for no reason. I picked up the magazines, left the clothes on the floor, and scooped up the lotion with, you guessed it, a baby wipe. I went back to the kitchen to return the blueberries to the refrigerator. When I opened the door, I bumped my elbow on the counter and dumped the entire container of blueberries all over the kitchen floor. You can't make this stuff up. I grudgingly picked them all up, put them back in the container and put them right back into the fridge.

This is what Monday looks like.

I used to feel bad for Monday. I used to think that it got a bad rap and that it was, at best, an excuse for another cup of coffee and, at worst, just a little misunderstood. But after today, I think it deserves every bit of its reputation. Monday, you are shaping up to be a real downer. And, if this Monday night rainstorm interferes with my satellite service and interrupts my regularly scheduled programming (read: The Bachelorette), we are going to have to rethink our relationship. I might just have to cut you out of my life entirely. Sorry Monday, it's not me, it's you.

# TEN STAGES OF BEDTIME

Remember when bedtime was as simple as climbing into bed and going to sleep? Perhaps you prepared for this restful renewal by sipping a warm cup of chamomile while you thumbed through the latest bestseller. Or maybe you snuggled up to your significant other on the couch and watched your favorite reality television series, unencumbered by interruptions. It's probably safe to say that whatever pre-bedtime rituals you practiced before the kids came along are nothing but memories now. (And, for some of us, the memories have been repressed by years of sleep deprivation and cold coffee.)

As I was putting the kids to bed tonight, I started thinking about how my pre-kid bedtime routine has been replaced by my post-kid bedtime circus show. One does not simply "go to bed" anymore. In fact, I think the bedtime situation at my house can best be described by breaking it down into ten distinct stages.

## Stage 1: Disbelief

The show begins as soon as the parent utters the phrase, "*Okay kids, time to get ready for bed.*" With the stage sufficiently set, the players now take their marks, ready to play their pre-assigned parts in what has become a nightly performance.

Frequently it is my eldest who assumes the lead role, exclaiming in disbelief, "*Wait, what? But it's still light outside? It's definitely not time for bed. I can't believe this. I just started watching this <insert YouTube Minecraft video>!*" All that is missing from his dramatic performance is an exclamation of "Oh, the humanity!" Then, auditioning for the Oscar in the category of Best Supporting Actress, our daughter chimes in with, "*We don't even go to bed until 8:00. Wait, what time is it? (7:58) See! It's not time, it's not time!*"

## Stage 2: The Grand Bargain

Feeling empowered by their newfound camaraderie, the siblings now make an attempt to offer up a solution – a compromise, if you will.

Kids: "*How about this mom, if you let us stay up for 10 more minutes, we promise to be extra good tomorrow and we will even clean up the toy room when we wake up. Just ten more minutes? Just until this grown woman on my video opens up the last colored egg to reveal what plastic toy hides inside?*" Okay, they don't say that last part, but, honestly, how (weirdly) brilliant is that lady? Do you know she makes six-figures from those videos? I am in the wrong business.

**Stage 3: Famine**

I'm not a scientist, but I have a hypothesis that the word "bedtime" triggers the hypothalamus to go into overdrive in children, alerting them to the danger of their impending starvation. It doesn't matter if they housed an entire Tombstone pizza for dinner an hour earlier, bedtime famine is an affliction that doesn't respond to reason. As a mother (or father), what are we to do here? Do we send our children to bed hungry, satisfied in the righteousness of our no-snacks-before-bedtime crusade? Or do we give in to their sad little faces and the thoughts of their empty tummies, growling in the darkness of their bedrooms. I'll save you the suspense about what happens in my household. Most nights I find myself pouring bowls of cereal at 7:59 and saying things like, "*This is the last time I'm doing this!*" and "*You should've eaten more of your dinner like I told you to!*" I can't take the thought of children going to bed hungry, be it real or imagined. One of these days I'll call their bluff, probably.

## Stage 4: The Long March

Sufficiently nourished, they are now required to physically move in the direction of their domiciles. In our house, this stage is characterized by a slow, methodic trudge up the stairs followed by an even slower shuffle step to the bathroom. Once inside, drawers will be pulled out, toothbrushes and toothpaste will be retrieved and the poor, tortured souls will half-heartedly commence the ritualistic cleansing of their sugar laced teeth. Most nights they won't even attempt to reach for a hand towel to dry off their faces after brushing. Instead, they will lumber down from their stools, water dripping from their chins, and look at me with eyes that seem to say, "Why bother?" Heads hung low in defeat; they retreat to their bedrooms.

## Stage 5: Last Requests and Lost Items

Inevitably, my son will forget to bring up a glass of water or my daughter will forget her Elsa pillow downstairs. These minor inconveniences are annoying, but easily remedied. On rare occasions, however, the worst possible scenario plays out during this stage. A situation so dire, so tragic, that it causes me to shudder just thinking about it. What circumstance could necessitate such a drastic response; you ask? Answer: The disappearance of Turtle Friend. This green and brown stuffed animal has cuddled with my son since his birth and sleep simply will not come if the two are separated. We've tried. It was a long, sad night and one that I don't wish to repeat any time soon. Whenever Turtle Friend is missing from my son's bedroom, we send out a search party to look high and low. No couch cushion is left unturned until this reptilian creature is returned to its rightful owner.

## Stage 6: Confessional

After the last page is read and the last sip of water is granted, I am magically transformed from a mother into a Catholic priest. My children, with their sweet hearts and innocent minds, feel the need to confess all of their sins of the day to me before they drift off into dreamland. It is during this time of night that I hear admissions of guilt such as, "*Remember when you told me to put the M&Ms away today? After you left the kitchen, I snuck into the pantry to eat a couple more. I'm sorry Mama.*" Or "*I broke my green crayon today and then I put it back into the box without telling you. I'm sorry Mama.*" I'm not going to lie, I'm a bit concerned about how these topics might progress as they get older.

## Stage 7: Random Questions

With clean consciences, my children are free to move on to the most entertaining stage of the night

– random question time. Some of my recent favorites include gems such as: *"Who do you think would win in a head-butting contest, me or Uncle Brenny?"* or, *"What is 64 times 232?"* I usually don't know how to answer these questions and the topics swing wildly from school related items such as, *"Do you know that a spider carries its eggs on its back?"* to more, shall we say, anatomical queries such as, *"But, how did the baby get OUT of your tummy?"*

## Stage 8: One More Hug

Feeling the lure of the downstairs DVR and the recliner calling my name, I tuck them into bed and kiss their soft little cheeks. I know that I will be called back to their bedsides for an encore performance of one last hug or one last kiss before I can make my exit. I don't mind this; in fact I hope for this. Even on my worst nights, after a tiring day of changing diapers and correcting behaviors, I purposely pause before reaching the threshold of their rooms, wishing for a little voice to beckon me for another embrace. Because one day they won't call out for one last hug. One day, probably too soon for my liking, they will simply say, *"Goodnight Mom,"* roll back over, and fall asleep. Their long arms will only reach out for one hug, and their teenage sensibilities will no longer allow for a kiss. But thankfully, that day is not today. Tonight, my daughter requires each and every variation of hug and kiss that she has discovered or created over the years: kiss, butterfly kiss, fish kiss, noozle, blow kiss, hug, bear hug, kitty snuggle, blow hug…and in that order.

## Stage 9: The Waiting Game

And then we wait. We tiptoe downstairs and wait for a head to pop out, uttering one last request or one last-ditch effort to squeeze out a few more sleep free minutes. We wait to see if their time in their beds is a permanent state or a temporary one. We wait to see if we can press play on our pre-recorded show that we are already days behind on watching. As we pick up the clothes, the toys, and the dirty plates, we listen, and we wait. And, finally, assured of their slumber, we get ready to go to bed too, content in the knowledge that we made it through another day of parenthood relatively unscathed.

## Stage 10: Did I Do Enough?

In the minutes (and sometimes hours) that precede our own sleep, we venture through the very last stage of bedtime. We replay our day and analyze and second-guess all our decisions. It is in these quietest of moments that we wonder – Am I doing enough? Are they warm enough? Did I pack enough food in their lunchbox? Did I give them enough attention? Did I tell them I loved them enough?

We know the answers, yet we still ask ourselves the questions - night after night, year after year. Do you know why we ask ourselves these questions? It's because we know that the days are long, but the years are short. We are painfully aware of the fleeting nature of time. We know that we won't always be the last ones to kiss them goodnight. So, despite our own fatigue and frustrations, we climb the stairs to reunite a lost stuffed animal and a little boy, and we give a million kisses to a little girl in a princess nightgown, and we rock a baby until our arms go numb.

If there were a thousand stages of bedtime, we'd do that too.

# DO YOU ENJOY BEING A MOTHER?

This morning I watched my one-year-old put her yogurt squeezer into the trashcan all by herself. I then watched her walk into the other room to catch a few seconds of Mickey Mouse Clubhouse, deliberately walk back to the trash to retrieve her yogurt, take a few swigs, open the lid to deposit it once again, and then return to her regularly scheduled programming. She then repeated this process three times. Why didn't I stop her from using our refuse container as her own personal pantry? Because the first baby you survive, the second baby you parent, and the third baby—well, you just sit back and enjoy that one.

It took me a while to realize what most grandmothers already know to be true (and try to tell new mothers who aren't yet ready to listen): our children grow quickly and these moments, the silly and the mundane, are what make up a mother's internal hard drive. The crayon drawn murals on freshly painted walls, the sibling haircuts that require emergency trips to the salon, the well-timed tantrums in the middle of the mall—these are the private video clips that flicker through a mother's mind years later, causing a chuckle or a tear, although likely both. The exasperated sighs of tired mothers today will be replaced by the nostalgic sighs of well-rested mothers years from now, those who would gladly rewind time to clean up spilled yogurt and wipe off sticky hands.

This realization was hard won, a product of years spent parenting in the trenches. When I first started this job, I read all the books and I knew all the best methods. I strategized meal plans and scheduled nap times. I stressed over the perfect bottle (BPA free with eight billion removable parts to clean), purchased the specially formulated (and ridiculously overpriced) baby detergent, and wasted way too many hours pureeing homemade baby food. I was over prepared, over planned, and over thinking. I routinely spent two hours gathering up baby gear in preparation to leave the house. This merits repeating—it took me TWO HOURS of preparation time just to walk out the door. What was I even packing? Why did I think I needed all those things? Who brings a wipes warmer to a Christmas party? (cough, cough…this girl.)

Sometimes I can't help but laugh at the Mom I was seven years ago and compare her to the Mom I am today—the one who spends 10 seconds getting ready for an entire day on the town—just enough time to grab a handful of diapers, a few wipes, and a bag of goldfish. But, in addition to laughing, I also worry that the Mom I was seven years ago missed out on some moments that should have been savored. Should I have rocked him to sleep instead of putting him down in his crib? Should I have studied his expressions instead of studying the latest findings on vaccinations? Should I have focused more on the little things instead of worrying so much about the big things?

The answers to these questions are obvious. But the trouble with parenting is that is an experiential profession—you must learn as you go. And as is the case with most things in life, you can't really get a good look at something until you are removed from it by time. When the paintbrush is in your hand and your nose is pressed to the canvas, you can't truly see the glory of the masterpiece. But, with experience comes perspective. And, when you know better, you take a break from creating the art every once in a while to step back and appreciate its beauty. You put down the paintbrush, take a seat on the bench, and admire the view from the gallery.

This realization comes in little spurts. The daily grind of parenting can take its toll. There are days when I barely stumble over the finish line. Days that I don't enjoy a single moment. Days that I send my kids to bed with a rushed hug and a quick "I love you," only to race downstairs to prepare for the next day. But when the chores are finished and I finally collapse into bed, I am saddened by the wasted chances to savor the moments. In the stillness of the night, I regret these missed opportunities to watch my children grow up. Sometimes I sneak back upstairs to watch their little faces as they sleep, trying my best to memorize every little feature of a masterpiece that changes a little every day.

I had one of those gut-check moments today. I was sweeping the kitchen floor after a birthday party celebrating my now seven-year-old boy and five-year-old girl and the baby was following me around the kitchen and crying for me to pick her up. The floor was covered in crushed up chips and sticky cake crumbles and I was determined to finish the cleaning job, even if that meant ignoring her pleas for attention for another three minutes. As the octave level of her wails progressed, I let out a frustrated sigh, and put the broom down so that I could pick her up. My son and his friend were at the kitchen table and the friend, overhearing my exasperation, sweetly asked, "*Do you enjoy being a mother*?" And with that single question, I realized the ridiculousness of my mission and the futility of my frustration. I hugged the sweet baby in my arms, happy to be resting her head on my shoulder, and left the cleaning for later. I held her on the couch while I chatted with my daughter about her new art kit. I watched my son and his friend attempt a science experiment. I took the time to just enjoy them for the amazing children they are—and I took a few mental snapshots for later.

So, to answer her question, I love being a mother. I love it even when it's hard. I love it even when my kids can't seem to go two minutes without fighting and must be sent to their rooms. I love it even when my house is a mess, and the dishes are piled high in the sink, and I can't see the bottom of the laundry basket. I love it in spite of all the responsibilities and uncertainties. I love it even when I have to remind myself to love it.

I didn't rush through the bedtime hugs tonight. I listened intently as both big kids recounted their favorite parts of the day. I rocked the baby to sleep and kept rocking her long after she drifted off into dreamland. I left the dishes in the sink and the broom against the kitchen wall. I enjoyed the moments that I'll never get back. One day I'll tell the baby about the time that she kept her lunch stored safely in the trashcan. Until then, I'll keep enjoying the memories in the making and I'll wipe off sticky hands and faces for as long as I can.

# PUT DOWN THE LAUNDRY BASKET

*"Mama, will you get to play with me today?"*

I probably get asked this question, or some version of it, an average of twelve times per day. My default answer usually involves an apologetic denial combined with an excuse meant to legitimize my response. My decline to an invitation to play tends to sound something like this - "*Sorry buddy, I have laundry to fold*" or "*Not right now, I'm making lunch*" or "*Maybe later, after I put the dishes away.*"

So why did this common request cause me to think twice before repeating my same old refrain today? Because of those two little words that he included this time—"*get to.*" It was as if he thought that some outside force was forbidding me to play, as if someone or something other than myself made the final decision. To my seven-year-old boy, this was the only plausible explanation. Because why would a mom ever turn down an invitation to spend quality time with her son if the decision were hers alone to make?

Turns out he was right. There was some outside force keeping me from saying yes to a round of Uno or a game of catch. This outside force, otherwise known as my To-Do List, consumes my time at home and habitually rents out space in my brain. Somewhere along the way, I'd allowed myself to become "too busy" to play. I chose laundry over laughter and making dinner over make believe. And I'd opted for order instead of the chaos created by play so many times that it had become our new normal: Mommy can't play – there's too much to do today.

I am an educator by trade, so I know this to be true—play is ESSENTIAL to learning. Albert Einstein once said, *"Play is the highest form of research."* The warmly sweatered Mr. Rogers added, *"Play gives children a chance to practice what they are learning."* The problem was that I was putting this theory to practice in my classroom but forgetting to continue it with my own children at home. In my most important role, that of my children's primary educator, I was failing to help them practice their learning. Luckily for me, they are persistent in their requests. Thankfully, I realized the missed opportunity before they gave up on me.

So, today I devoted an entire day to play and I was amazed by the results. In my research I found that my son doesn't need me to keep score in Scrabble anymore. I learned that my daughter is an expert on spiders, as she demonstrated by answering a trivia question meant for an adult and then enlightening all of us on five different varieties of spiders, how they carry their babies, the placement of their eyes, and the markings on their bodies. And, most surprisingly, I discovered that my baby knows the color blue. Turns out her Nana knows the importance of play in learning and has been teaching her colors while playing with blocks. We could learn a thing or two from grandparents—they are never too busy to play.

In my constant crusade to check off items on my chore list, I'd missed the most important tasks of all—to play and discover, to engage and explore. But I won't make that mistake again. From now on, play gets a spot on the To-Do List. The blankets will be folded after the Queen conquers the fort. The vacuum will just have to wait its turn. We have more important things to do than the dishes. There are more pressing matters that demand my immediate attention—like the soldiers advancing with Nerf guns on my precarious position in the closet or this tower of mega blocks on the brink of destruction by Babyzilla. So, if you'll excuse me, I must put down my laptop—there is lava spewing over my living room floor and my only chance for survival is to jump to safety and join my children on Red Couch Island.

# LIFE BEFORE KIDS

I woke this morning nose-to-nose with a cute little blonde repeating my name with increasing frequency. Her blue eyes were inches from mine and her chubby toddler fingers were tapping my forehead to reassure me that this was not a drill. Her message was clear, and her demands were specific—chocolate milk and Paw Patrol, STAT! In dragging my perpetually tired 30-something body out of bed to lumber to the kitchen, I realized that there are certain things I took for granted in my life before I had kids. Simple things like sleeping past 7:00 on a Sunday morning, eating a hot meal when it is served, and visiting the restroom without an audience. As all parents can attest, life after kids is a brave new world, one that requires a complete overhaul of all previous norms, routines, and expectations. It's a little foggy in this new world (sleep deprivation will do that) and it's sometimes difficult to remember what the pre-kid planet looked like, but I'll do my best to compare the seismic shift that occurs after the happiest day of your life.

## Weekend Mornings

Remember when a Saturday morning meant waking around 11:00 to a hot cup of coffee and a crossword puzzle in bed? Perhaps you would join friends for a brunch buffet and partake in a tomato-infused drink with a piece of celery and a little kick. The biggest decision before noon would be whether to catch up on your Netflix shows or go to Yoga class. Either choice would be fine, since you had the rest of the day ahead of you to complete the other one. The morning was slow and lazy and all yours.

Fast forward a kid or two and that hot cup of coffee now needs to be rewarmed in the microwave every half hour or so. Waking up at 11:00? Please, by that time of day you've already made breakfast, cleaned up spilled cheerios on the carpet, changed three diapers, folded a load of laundry, watched four episodes of Doc McStuffins, refereed a fight over an iPad, and are busily preparing a lunch that nobody will eat.

## Weekend Nights

And since we're talking about the weekends, remember those late Saturday nights filled with music and friends and reckless abandon? Checking out a new club at midnight and catching a cab home at 2:30 was the norm. Summer nights were filled with endless possibilities and limited only by the crowd and never by the clock. After a long work week, Saturday night was freedom at its finest and the party didn't need to end until the sun came up because the next day could be completely devoted to rest and recovery.

But the weekends are a little different with little feet running around. If the day has been spent at the ballpark, the night will be filled with baths and cereal for dinner. If you enjoyed a fun afternoon at the beach, the night will be filled with baths and cereal for dinner. If the kids ran around with cousins at the extended family cookout, the night will be filled with…you guessed it…baths and cereal for dinner. And, with any luck, this all happens before 9:00 p.m. Staying up until midnight? Now that's just crazy talk.

## Going Out to Eat

In the six years before I had children, I made dinner reservations with the same frequency as most people make their beds. I tried all kinds of restaurants: barbecue joints and fondue bistros, breakfast cafes and hole-in-the-wall bars. I ordered appetizers and savored the entrees and spent hours talking with friends over candlelight and sampling the dessert special. My food was always hot, my drinks were always fresh, and the floor beneath my table was always clean.

I still go out to eat now, but more out of necessity and a bad case of amnesia regarding the last three trips to the restaurant. The dining establishment must meet a strict set of criteria: 1. Family friendly (chicken strip kid's meals and high-chairs), 2. Cost effective (chances are they won't eat their food anyway), and 3. Close to home (in case of a melt-down or diaper mishap). If they give out crayons they get bonus points, if they don't have chocolate milk they get crossed of the list. I appreciate the fact that I do not have to prepare any of the meals but going out to eat still does not absolve me from cutting up pancakes, eating cold food, and picking strands of spaghetti out of the carpet.

## Sitting Down

This is the one thing that I took for granted the most. Plopping myself on the couch for an hour or two without interruption. Sitting down at my desk to work on a project and only rising from my seat when I needed to refresh my diet coke.

I don't really remember what it was like to just sit down. Because sitting down now is the universal signal for my kids to ask me for something. The water cup needs refilled when my backside touches the recliner, the baby needs changed as soon as I put my feet up on the chaise lounge, the pink crayon goes missing the moment I park myself on the loveseat. I like to call these moments Mom Squats. They make up for my morning run I've missed the last 52 consecutive days.

## Laundry

Before kids, it was typical to have a "laundry day." Usually a Sunday, this was the day devoted to getting the two or three loads of laundry that had accumulated over the week washed and folded and put away. It was a task with a definite end, one that could be completed within a few hours and forgotten about until next week.

But now, every day is "laundry day." Actually, that isn't correct. Every day SHOULD be laundry day in order to keep up with the massive piles of onesies and colorful socks and baseball pants. But in our house, it just tends to build up to a critical mass every week until I break down and attempt to scale the mountain of miniature t-shirts and make a dent in the cotton-based peaks and valleys on my bedroom floor. Sometimes I manage to get them all put away (at least for a few hours), but usually I just fold them and place them in a basket to be rifled through in the morning rush of the coming days.

## Everything Else

To be sure, I had more energy and free time before my three little ones came along. Before they arrived, my steak was always hot, and my lemonade was always cold. And there is no doubt that binge watching the Sopranos beat any marathon of Mickey Mouse Clubhouse. But I've found the sweetness of a two-year-old calling me Mommy far outweighs the solitude of just being Stacey. And even though I must share everything now—my french fries, my blankets, and my love—the return on investment is worth the price of my privacy. I'll take early mornings and early nights over the way it used to be, because the way it used to be was missing a few things anyway. It was missing the heartfelt conversations of bedtime with three little monkeys snuggled up beside me. It was missing the pride and the tears that accompany the big moments—the first steps, the first day of school, the first base hit. It was missing the depth of love that can only be felt when a piece of you is transformed into another individual, one that comes into this world and changes yours forever.

# HOW DO YOU DO IT ALL?

*"I don't know how you do it all!"*

Within the past week, I've had this phrase thrown in my direction by four different friends in four different contexts. One friend said it regarding my complicated weekend schedule that involved multiple sporting events for my children mixed in with household projects and real estate appointments. Another said it in jest, as a response to a post on Facebook where I intimated that I needed to partake in an adult beverage before tackling the mountain of laundry cascading over my couch. Yet another said it in a private conversation when I shared my desire to write a book amongst other projects that I have piled on my plate. And, lastly, one friend said it as a compliment but, in doing so, minimized her importance as a mother because she assumed that she should be able to accomplish the same tasks considering she *"only has one kid and stays at home all day."*

So, I'm here to tell you my secret. It's time to pull back the curtain to reveal just how I "*do it all.*" The answer is simple really.

I don't.

I don't do it all. Not even close. Behind each weekly article is a tired Mom lying in bed with an open laptop and a handful of thin mints. For every event that we manage to make it to on time are three others that we are fashionably late for. (And by fashionably, I mean the kind where we show up 15 minutes past the tardy bell because our morning included me demanding the kids to "*get your butts in the car and I don't care if you can't find your coat because I told you ten minutes ago to look for it but you were too busy watching Stampy Cat on YouTube to listen to me so now you will just have to run really fast at recess to stay warm.*") For every educational moment filled with love and understanding are two maddening moments filled with frustration and despair. And every parenting win is balanced out by an equally emotional (and sometimes epic) fail.

Nobody does it all. And if they claim to have it all under control, they are lying (to you and to themselves). Mr. Storm, my high school social studies teacher, taught me that economics is all about trade-offs and opportunity costs. I think the same theory could be applied to life in general. For every choice that we make, there is one that we didn't. Every time I take my kids to hockey practice, I choose to replace a family dinner spent around our kitchen table with a microwaved corndog from the concession stand. Every time I stay up late to write a blog, I decrease the likelihood that I will drag myself out of bed early the next morning to spend some quality time with my treadmill. Every time I choose to snuggle my baby in the rocking chair, I decide to postpone the removal of the thin layer of dust decorating the flat surfaces of my living room for another day.

I'll just give you a brief synopsis of the past week to illustrate my point. Anybody looking in from the outside would've considered the week a smashing success: I wrote an article for one of my jobs and four offers for another; I took my two girls shopping at the mall and my oldest girl enjoyed a lovely evening at her school's Daddy/Daughter dance; I attended the Winterfest basketball game at my local high school; I successfully managed to get two kids to five practices and three games with the third kid in tow; I enjoyed an evening out painting and chatting with girlfriends; I put all of the freshly washed clothes away in their respective spots in closets and dressers; and I kept up to date with the latest information on the presidential race.

Now, behind-the-scenes, the reality of last week dispels any notion that I "*do it all*." That

article was written on a laptop sitting on my kitchen
counter in between stirring the hamburger meat and
feeding goldfish to a clingy toddler hanging from
my leg. That trip to the mall occurred far later into
the night than any respectable mother should have
her kids out and ended with a rushed trip through
the Chick-Fil-A drive-thru on the way home for a
nutritious dinner of French fries and ketchup. To
get through most of the basketball game, I had to
bribe my aforementioned clingy toddler with a bag
of M&Ms and a sucker, which turned out to be a
terrible idea later that night when the sugar in her
system convinced her that she shouldn't be forced
to go to bed. On the way home from one of the five
hockey practices, my middle child dumped an entire
bottle of blue Gatorade on the floor of my used-to-
be-new van and then looked at me for direction
while the sticky liquid created a wading pool on the
carpet. And that night out with the girls? That
involved some fancy maneuvering of our schedules
and babies left at home crying for their mamas.
And let's not forget the brand-new shoes that were
purchased during our trip to the mall. On Monday, I
inadvertently scooped one of them up with a pile of
clothes and sent it through the washing machine,
causing my toddler to go out in public dressed as
Shoeless Joe Jackson. On Wednesday, I did it again.

So, whether you have four kids or fur babies, a
full-time career or a stay-at-home gig, it is

impossible to "*do it all.*" I'm coming up on my 35th year of life in a couple of months and the most important lesson I've learned on this journey so far is that we can only do what we can do, and the rest will just have to wait. We are all so strikingly similar in our desire to do more and be more. But sometimes I wonder if, in our quest for perfection and our tendency to compare, we fail to notice the commonality of the human experience. We are all juggling schedules and prioritizing time, kissing our babies and leaving for work, ordering take-out and skipping the gym. We are all doing enough if we are doing what we can. You won't find SuperMom in my house. Besides, her uniform is a little too snug since the third kid and her cape was recommissioned as a burp cloth years ago.

# TELL ME ABOUT YOUR DAY

The best part of my day happens every evening between 7:45 and 8:00 p.m. For the last seven years, I've spent the fifteen minutes before bedtime lying next to my pajama-clad children and asking them to tell me about their day. I don't check my phone, I don't impart any wisdom, I don't even interject very much—I just listen. Oh, the wonderful things you can learn if you just listen.

Of course, this is not a new idea. Moms and dads have enjoyed the soft chatter of their children before bedtime for eons. Any parent will tell you they learn all sorts of things from their babies in the whispered conversations just moments before they drift off to sleep. My Mom used to tuck my sister and I into bed every evening and sit on the edge of it for a while to listen as we shared our stories and adventures from the day. We would tell her about our travels on Space Pig (the propane tank in the yard that doubled as a pork-themed rocket ship) and attempt to explain the newest make-believe game played that day with Grandma Sears at "Baby Work" (old-fashioned daycare—the kind where the grandma watches all of the cousins). It was in these precious moments before bed that my little sister would confess all of her sins of the day to my mom. Forget trying to keep a secret about a broken vase or a missing glove, any minor slip-ups during the day would spill out of my sister's mouth at night and the jig was up. No wonder she always slept so soundly—a clear conscience provides a restful night.

Many years later, I carried on this tradition with my first-born. As soon as he was able to talk, I would ask him all sorts of questions before he closed his eyes. He caught on quickly to the routine, and would snuggle into his toddler bed and ask, "*Mama, talk about our day?*" He would go on to tell me about the popsicle his Grandpa Steve snuck him when his Grandma Jan wasn't looking, the walk he took with his grandma's dog Zoe, and the new trick he learned on his tricycle. It didn't matter if it wasn't Friday, her day to watch him, he always told me that he went to Grandma Jan's that day. The bond those two shared was magical—they were thick as thieves and loved every second of each other's company. Just a few months after his little sister was born and one month after his second birthday, his Grandma Jan passed away on

Christmas morning. As anyone who has ever lost a parent knows, the tragedy of this event was almost unbearable. But the sadness of the days that followed was lifted for a few minutes every night as I listened to my sweet boy tell me about the adventures that he shared with his Grandma Jan that day. It didn't matter if he was recounting old tales from months ago; I loved listening to his memories and wished they would last forever. I like to believe that they still meet up in his dreams at night to take Zoe for a walk and share popsicles and popcorn.

Lately, I've added a new twist to the bedtime routine. A couple of weeks ago I saw an article on Facebook titled, *"Three Questions to Ask Your Child Every Night."* I love the conversations that result from these simple prompts and my kids can't wait to snuggle up on their pillows and give me their answers. Here are the three questions if you'd like to give it a try:

1. What is something that made you happy today?
2. What is something that made you sad today?
3. What is something that you learned today?

Their answers to these questions reveal so much more than their successes and setbacks of the day. I've discovered that my kids are in love with their new music teacher who has, according to my son, *"the most beautiful voice in the world."* I learned that my daughter likes to chase a certain little boy on the playground and had the "*best time ever*" during a recent sleepover. I never know where these questions will take us. Last night my son said that he heard on the radio that people were voting in a primary and he wanted to know what that meant. I spent the next ten minutes explaining the presidential election process and describing the differences between Republicans and Democrats. Always the Analyzer-in-Chief, he wrapped up our discussion by declaring, "*I know what Grandma Dodson is then…she always takes care of animals, she likes peace instead of guns, and she LOVES Hillary Clinton…she must be a Democrat.*"

I like to think that our nightly discussions are laying the groundwork for open lines of communication that will be essential during their teenage years. I'm sure I will learn of countless crushes and heartbreaks this way, and I hope that when that time comes, I will have the wisdom to just listen instead of trying to "fix" every problem that comes their way. With any luck, I will discover their fears and their aspirations by sitting at the foot of their beds. Armed with that knowledge, maybe I can help them work through their doubts and encourage their ambitions. If nothing else, I know that when my hair is gray and my nest is empty, I will look back at these little moments and smile, knowing that they were actually the big moments.

# SLOW DOWN, YOU'RE GOING TO MISS IT

Sometimes, you just hit a wall.  Sometimes you just need to step back, take a breath…and then take a break.  This is a hard thing to admit and an even more difficult sentence to write.  Yet, despite all the self-reminders to "enjoy the moment" and to not "sweat the small stuff," sometimes the enormity of adult life is just too much.

The feeling doesn't hit all at once. It is a slow process that starts with a dull sense of dread, like the knock of an unwanted guest at your door.  You try to hide behind the curtains, remain silent and avoid any sudden movements, in the hopes that your unwelcomed visitor will vacate the premises and leave you to your normal routine.   But dread is a persistent caller. It's silhouette casts a long shadow, and it intends to stay on your porch, rocking in your chair until you unlock the screen door and let it inside.  Dread can take many forms.

It can make you call in sick and impair your motivation. It can cause your feet to drag and your excuses to formulate. It can make you respond with a sigh to requests of "*Just one more book!*" and "*Look at me Mommy!*" It isn't acute by nature, but it's there nonetheless…just below the skin, poisoning your productivity and ravaging your resolve.

Once inside, dread morphs into frustration and defies rational thought. Mundane tasks become mountainous. Sighs are accompanied by shouts. They shouldn't be. I know this. You know this. A request for another glass of water is just that. Until it isn't. Until the trek downstairs to fetch yet another receptacle of liquid is just the latest in an endless line of demands that started at 6:00 a.m. with the correct color of cereal bowl, continued with the urgent email wanting an immediate reply, moved on to the homework that required a signature, and kept on going to the search for a lost stuffed kitten. Sometimes that second glass of water takes on a whole new meaning and its retrieval might as well be a hike across the Gobi Desert. Yes, sometimes logic loses its mind.

After the frustration dies down (usually after the natives have gone to bed), regret soon takes its place. The irrational responses and missed opportunities play on a loop in your head as you wipe a tear or two away and pick up the now empty sippy cups.  The regret is a familiar feeling.  It is an old friend, the quiet kind who sits in the corner, crocheting a scarf and throwing out age-old adages like "*It's not a race.*" or "*If you don't slow down, you're going to miss it.*"

Its days like these I ponder the purpose of trying to do it all.  I ask myself questions like, "*Why did you take on that project when you know you don't have the time?*" or "*Why did you agree to another activity when it means another night of drive-thru dinners in the car?*"  I feel the heavy load of a full-time career, a full-time parenting gig, and not enough hours in the day.  I look at the dishes piled in the sink and the three-day-old layer of crumbs scattered on the floor, remnants of rushed meals and skipped chores, and think—"*Does it really have to be this hard?*"  I know the answer.  But my problem lies in the implementation of the truth.

Despite the mantra of my millennial upbringing to do more and be more, I crave a simpler time with a slower pace. I want to teleport back to the 50s, throw on an apron, and bake some dang cookies. I wish there were more days spent wearing hiking boots and fewer days wearing high heels. There are days when I curse my profession and question my choices.  When I pick up my sleeping baby from a warm bed and transfer her to a cold car seat to drop her off with a caregiver before the sun comes up, I wonder if the benefits outweigh the costs. When I race back and forth between meetings and appointments, practices and commitments, I can physically feel the futility of the effort and the exhaustion of the rat race. It is at the end of those days, when my hair is frazzled and my to-do list is still too long, that I want to scream out – Enough, enough already!

And then I hit the proverbial wall. The wall that is there to knock you down and make you see stars and force you to take a time-out for your sanity. The wall that whispers, "*Just stay down there and rest for a little while...watch a little Netflix and snuggle up with your babies. The world will keep turning and the sun will come up tomorrow. "Progress" can wait another day.*

There has to be a better way. Life cannot be a series of races and crashes. How did we get to the point where our schedules are so full that we can't fit in a day in our pajamas or regular dinners around the table? I haven't watched a movie that isn't made by Pixar in close to five years. I haven't slept past 9:00 in seven years. (Okay, that's because I have three kids, so I brought that one on myself.) I have become so used to the fast pace of modern life that I've forgotten how to get off the treadmill and just stand still.

So, I'm making a vow, to my family and myself, to slow it down. I promise to say no to outside distractions and yes to quality interactions. When I see the wall approaching, I'm not going to keep my foot on the pedal and encourage a head-on collision. I'm going to act rationally—let off the gas and apply pressure to the brake. I'm not going to scream out in angst or take out my frustrations on those I love. Because, despite the difficulty of the job, I am an adult. Because the bills will still be there after my tantrum. Because there are three little faces upstairs that are thirsty for water and desperate for another story.

# CLASS DISMISSED

There was no easy way to tell you. I had been rehearsing my speech in my head for a week and my stomach churned with a mixture of dread and guilt as you entered my classroom Monday morning. I was leaving you. After all the progress made and the relationships formed, I was stepping down as your teacher and wouldn't be returning for the second semester. As I looked at your shocked faces, tears streaming down your cheeks, I couldn't even make it through the first sentence without breaking down myself. You are my kids, and I am leaving you—and for that I am deeply sorry.

I didn't intend for our journey to end this way. Following my year-long maternity leave last year, I excitedly returned to teaching this past fall and thought I would pick up right where I left off and continue my career path, full-steam ahead. I spent hours decorating my new classroom with Pinterest inspired ideas and colorful patterns. I revamped my curriculum and changed up my materials to reflect the changing demands and interests of your generation. I planned our entire year down to the day and wrote it all out on a color-coded calendar. I thought I could do it all. Teaching full time and being a full-time mom of three little kids wouldn't be so difficult. Or so I thought.

And then October rolled around and my sweet kindergartner asked me if I could attend her field trip to the pumpkin patch. And my son asked if I could volunteer to help at his Halloween party. I desperately wanted to, but there was just one problem: I had a classroom to run during that time and I couldn't just leave my own classroom to go to another. You see, a teacher's schedule is a great schedule for a mom. You get to spend your summers and seasonal school breaks with your family, not to mention the bonus of snow days. But you miss out on a bunch of other stuff. Important stuff. Because my first class starts before my kids are even awake, my daughter's hairstyle on picture day was left for someone else to figure out. Because my 4th hour is during my son's lunchtime, I had to decline the invitation to attend his Thanksgiving Feast. Sure, I saw how much fun he had in the images posted on Facebook by other mothers, but these are moments that just don't translate well through pictures. And then, on November 21, I picked him up from school and, with a shaky voice and watery eyes, he asked me why I didn't send in birthday treats to his classroom that morning. The truth is, I'd forgotten all about it. I'd been so busy grading papers the night before and running from one practice to the next that I'd dropped the ball on his special day. And that was it. My son's 7th birthday was the day I decided that I couldn't do it all. If I wanted to be the best mother I could be to my children, I had to be more present and not preoccupied with an all-consuming career. I had to find a different path that would allow me the flexibility to play a more prominent role in all aspects of their lives. I wanted to be there *with* them, and I wanted to be there *for* them. And that's why I can't stay here with you.

You might not understand this now, and that's okay. One day, when you have little ones of your own, you will realize just how fast the time flies. You will know why I want to grab every second of time I have with them. You will understand the ache I feel in my heart when I look at the clock on my classroom wall and realize that I am missing yet another morning with my babies. For nine months out of the year, I don't get to be the one who rubs their tiny backs to wake them up or hear their little voices call out, "*Mama*?" as they slowly make their way down the stairs. For nine months out of the year, I take care of other peoples' children during the day while somebody else takes care of mine. That idea just doesn't make sense to me anymore.

Please don't think this was an easy decision. In fact, it was the hardest decision I've ever had to make. Throughout the course of the year, you have become my children too. I carry your challenges home with me, and I've spent many sleepless nights pondering possible solutions or scheming up ways to help you achieve your goals. I think about your futures and worry about any roadblocks that might come your way. I celebrate your accomplishments and cheer you on in the stands. I admire your talents and strengths and pray that you realize your full potential.  I treasure your quirkiness, I laugh at your silly jokes, and I love your awkwardness. I am your biggest fan...and that will never change.

So, in the short time we have left, I wanted to leave you with a few parting lessons. No, there won't be a key terms quiz or an essay test to follow and answering in paragraph format and complete sentences won't be necessary this time. I know how you love my dynamic lectures (cough, cough)…so here are the last section of notes I will leave you with:

1.  You were born to be great. Don't let anybody tell you otherwise. It takes all types of talents to run the world and I've seen what you can do when you put your mind to it.

2. There is going to come a time when you are faced with a decision. When that time comes, you might be too scared to take a chance. Do it anyway. Life is too short to live with regret and that limb you're going out on is stronger than you think.

3. Action cures anxiety. If you are nervous about a speech or anxious about a test, the fastest way to relieve that feeling is to take a deep breath and begin. I know it sounds counterintuitive, but you have to trust me on this one. Just get out of your head and get it done.

4. You wouldn't care so much about what people thought of you if you knew how seldom they really did. Everyone is too busy living their own lives to obsess about your new hairstyle or your lack of expensive shoes. I don't mean this to be harsh, I mean it to be freeing. Just remember: the people who mind don't matter, and the people who matter don't mind.

5. Don't believe people who tell you that these are the best years of your life. It gets better…so much better.

6. Tell people you love them. Sometimes we neglect to tell others how we feel about them because we are embarrassed, or we think they already know or we are worried the feelings won't be reciprocated. Get over this fear. If

there's one thing we need in this world it's more love.

7. You are a Buck. With that distinction comes a tremendous amount of pride and an enormous amount of responsibility. We are a Herd, thousands strong with roots that run deep. You carry the torch of the many who came before you and are tasked with continuing our traditions and carrying on our legacy. Never forget the strong foundation that was provided to you by a community that cares about you.

8. You are the leading role in the play of your life. Speak loudly. Move with a purpose. Show your emotions. Pause for laughs. And, most importantly, leave it all on the stage.

Well crew, that's all I have for you today. It's been a great run and the memories will last a lifetime. I look forward to reuniting at graduation parties and Homecoming games, wedding receptions, and baby showers. Thank you for strengthening my faith in your generation and teaching me that connections and relationships are the most important part of our educational process. If the future of our nation depends on you, I am confident that we are in good hands. I love every one of you and am honored to have been a small part of your lives. Keep in touch.

Class dismissed.

# ABOUT THE AUTHOR

Stacey Martin is a proud Buchanan Buck and host of "The Folks Back Home" podcast. With a background in education and marketing, Martin left the corporate world to pursue her dream of raising babies and being a writer. She spends her days going on adventures with her husband, chasing four little Bucks, and chronicling the stories of her beloved hometown.

Made in the USA
Monee, IL
24 October 2021